To my Godson
with Love

Robt. P Lawrie

Sept 1985

The Journal of Sir Peter Laurie

THE JOURNAL OF SIR PETER LAURIE

Costello, with the Saddlers' Company, 1985

Published in 1985

 All enquiries to:
D.J. Costello (Publishers) Ltd,
43 The High Street, Tunbridge Wells, Kent TN1 1XL.

British Library Cataloguing in Publication Data
Laurie, *Sir* Peter, *1778-1861*
Journal of Sir Peter Laurie
1. Laurie, *Sir* Peter, *1778-1861*
2. Saddlery
——Great Britain——Biography
I. Title
II. Saddlers' Company
338.7'6851'0924 TS1032

ISBN 0-7104-4000-6

Typeset by Composing Operations Ltd,
88a London Road, Southborough, Kent TN4 0PP.
Printed in Great Britain by J.W. Arrowsmith Ltd,
Winterstoke Road, Bristol BS3 2NT.
Bound in Great Britain by Green Street Bindery,
9 Green Street, Oxford OX4 1YB.

INTRODUCTION

Background

Sir Peter Laurie was born in 1778 at Sandersdean in the parish of Haddington, East Lothian. He was the twelfth and youngest child of John Laurie, a farmer, and the only son of Agnes Thomson, his father's second wife. The family lived on several farms in the neighbourhood of Stichill, including Queenscairn and Kedgley, before settling in Sandersdean. Peter Laurie began training for the Presbyterian Church under the influence of the Reverend John Brown, the minister of Haddington and a noted theological writer. However, his father's third wife was determined to clear the house of children and so, at the age of 12, Sir Peter was apprenticed to his brother George, a saddler in Jedburgh. Within three years he was sent home by the local magistrate after being beaten by his brother, and took up his apprenticeship in various Edinburgh shops, becoming a foreman in 1796.

Sir Peter's involvement in national politics, which began with his attending meetings of the 'Society of the Friends of the People', a reforming Whig group, precipitated his move to London. He had incurred his master's displeasure by leading a wages dispute and therefore decided he could advance better in London. So, with a little money and a few letters of reference, he travelled to London and eventually he found a position in Borough. In the next two years he worked his way up and in 1798 became foreman to David Pollock, the King's saddler.

Both in Edinburgh and in London Sir Peter's great interest, after his work, was drama. He took part in many private performances of plays by Shakespeare and others which led in 1800 to offers of engagements to play with a touring theatre company. His cousin George Aitchison and a friend of Sir Peter's, Mr Richards, prevented him from accepting these offers, which might have disgraced the family, by helping him to set up his own saddlery business. In 1801 he set up shop at 293 Oxford Street. By 1803 he was sufficiently secure financially to marry Margaret Jack whom he had met at Swallow Street chapel. Business was prospering as a result of Sir Peter's hard work and advantageous military contracts with the East India Company. By 1811 he had moved his shop to 296 Oxford Street. Sir Peter was now in a position to help his poorer relatives: in 1804 he sent his nephew John Snaddon to school and in 1811 he did the same for John's brother Peter, called Robert Peter. Later they were both apprenticed to him. He also paid for the education of his grand-nephew Alexander Reid. In 1810, he took into his household his nephew Peter Laurie, later Northall Laurie; he took in his grand-niece, Margaret Laurie, in 1845.

Sir Peter's first involvement in the work of charitable institutions was in 1815 when he became secretary to the 'Society in Scotland for Propagating Christian Knowledge' and treasurer of the 'Highland School Society'. He was also a member of Sir Samuel Romilly's reforming committees. By 1820 he had taken John into partnership and began to withdraw from active business. By the time Robert Peter became a partner in 1823, Sir Peter had retired from business, living first at Cornwall Terrace, NW, and moving three years later to 7 Park Square, Regent's Park.

In 1823 Sir Peter was elected Sheriff of the City of London, thus beginning an association with City Administration that was to continue until his death in 1861. As sheriff his main concern was for the treatment of prisoners, especially in Newgate, and he made reforms in hanging techniques. These interests no doubt influenced the governors of the Bridewell and Bethlem (Bethlehem) Hospitals to elect him president in 1833. Sir Peter became very interested in the systems of prison administration and was an advocate of George Chesterton's silent system, by which the prisoners were permitted to associate by day in silence. He introduced this system at Bridewell in opposition to the regime of solitary confinement practiced at Pentonville and Millbank*. Sir Peter wrote two pamphlets against the solitary system, 'Killing no murder' in 1846 and 'A letter on the disadvantages and extravagance of the separate system of prison discipline . . . to the Corporation . . .' in 1848. At Bethlehem Hospital he advocated reform along the lines of the more humane methods used at the Quaker Retreat near York, which he had visited in 1820. He was also a director of the Caledonian asylum.

The middle years of the nineteenth century were a period of great ferment in the City of London. In the wake of the Parliamentary Reform Act of 1832 and the moves to widen vestry election franchise, there were calls for radical reform of the City administration. A Royal Commission to examine municipal corporations resulted in an Act of 1835 to reform municipal administration. London was excluded from this Act, although not from the Commissioners' scrutiny. They finally reported on the City in 1837. Recognising the threat from outside, the Corporation made some reforms, although most aldermen and livery companies opposed anything that undermined their privileges†. Sir Peter had been an advocate of reform in his youth and still supported the reform of injustices; but he disliked the riots and the violence of some radicals, Chartists and Anti-Corn Law League members, and gradually became a tory. The question of reform of City administration was raised regularly in Parliament, by newspaper editorials and by public men, but no major changes were imposed on the City until the London County Council was formed, well after Sir Peter's death.

It was probably in 1822-3 that Sir Peter decided to begin his journal autobiography when he had achieved a position which, with an eye to posterity, he thought worthy of record. Sir Peter gives much useful information about commerce and administration in his account of his activities as sheriff, as alderman of Aldersgate ward, as Lord Mayor, as governor of the Union Bank and as a magistrate in Marylebone. As a liveryman and assistant and Master of the Saddlers' Company, Sir Peter notes practices of the Company including the election of liverymen to the Court of Assistants and the numbers of dinners held each year. In the 1830s the Saddlers' Company was one of the few Companies which still exercised a measure of control over its trade, undertaking searches for defective goods‡ and maintaining close links with the saddlery trade. These are illustrated in 1830 by the initial refusal of the Court to accept Peter Northall Laurie on the Livery because he had neither served an apprenticeship nor was he engaged in the trade of saddlery.

In this account of his life Sir Peter Laurie writes engagingly on a wide variety of topics from his Scottish boyhood and early theatrical interests, to his setting up of a saddlery business and his eminent position in City business affairs and administration in early Victorian London. His journal throws valuable light on each of these subjects, and many others, as well as being the interesting story of the rise of a capable and ambitious man.

The Journal and Editorial Principles

The journal is a single bound small folio volume containing 196 leaves. Eleven blank pages begin the volume, with 'Sir P. Laurie' pencilled on the eighth, followed by 357 pages of text in holograph, then 22 blank pages. There is no original pagination. This edition is a complete transcription of the original. One of two apparently contemporary insertions is transcribed here as Appendix A, originally two folded large folio sheets.

The journal appears to have been written up in retrospect and from memory until about 1822-3, then at regular intervals from diary notes although still in narrative form. By the middle of 1830 marginated dates divide the entries and since this practice becomes consistent from January 1831.

All headings used in this edition were marginations in the original text or, in the case of year dates, were placed at the head of the page. All punctuation and capitals have been modernized without comment and all abbreviations extended. Numerals and fractions are reproduced as they stand in the original. The original spelling has been retained. All editorial additions are enclosed in round brackets.

The volume has remained in the Laurie family and is now held by R.P. Laurie, of Brentwood, Essex. There is a photocopy in the Guildhall Library London. Manuscripts department, reference MS. 20,334.

Related Documents

There are a number of documents related to the journal. Sir Peter refers to his Lett's diaries for the first time in 1823, suggesting he kept his appointments diary separately. Peter Northall Laurie's travel journals and newspaper cutting books are referred to. In his mayoral year Sir Peter's invitation book and the court journal are mentioned. All of these are now lost, as far as is known.

Sir Peter also published some pamphlets:

1. Substance of the speech of Sir Peter Laurie on the question of the periodical election of magistrates in the Court of Common Council, 28th March 1835 (London 1835).
2. Narrative of proceedings at the laying of the first stone at Bridewell (London, July 1838).
3. Observation on the report to the Court of Common Council from the Election Act committee (London, 1843)
4. Speech at the public breakfast of the Wesleyan Missionary Society (London, 1843)
5. Killing no murder, or the effects of separate confinement on the . . . condition of prisoners . . . (London, 1746)
6. A letter on the disadvantages and extravagance of the separate system of prison discipline . . . addressed to the Corporation of the City of London (London, 1848)

Attributed to him are:

7. Carmen ante pastum, or the preliminary praises of the coming mayoralty- . . . (London, 1832)
8. Maxims of Sir Peter Laurie . . . Lord Mayor of London . . . (London, 1833)

Sir Peter's life is recounted in Peter G. Laurie's *Sir Peter Laurie, a family memoir* (London, 1901), which has an appendix of family trees. He is mentioned in the *Dictionary of National Biography*, XI, 651-2; in *Townsend's Calendar of Knights*; in *City Press*, (7 December 1861); in the *Gentleman's Magazine* (January 1862), pt i pp 91-3; in James Grant's *Portraits of Public Characters* (London, 1841); and in John W. Sherwell's *A History of the guild of Saddlers of the city of London*, revised by K.S. Laurie (London 1956). An article by J.M. Russell, 'East Lothian's Dick Whittington' is in *The Scots Magazine* for May 1980 (vol. 113, no 2, p.202-6). There were numerous obituaries in 1861 in newspapers including *The Times, Morning Advertiser* and *Observer*. Dickens is said to have based the character of Alderman Cute in *The Chimes* on that of Sir Peter.

There do not appear to be any other publications of journals of Lord Mayors of London except William Purdie Treloar, *A Lord Mayor's Diary, 1906-7, to which is added the official diary of Micajah Perry, Lord Mayor 1738-9,* (London, 1920). A number of manuscripts of similar mayoral diaries, including that of Perry mentioned above, and of Kelly (Lord Mayor 1836-7), are kept in the Guildhall Library London, Manuscripts department. These are generally little more than offical appointment books; however John Fryer, Lord Mayor 1720-1, wrote a longer autobiographical account.

Portraits

Sir Peter Laurie mentions sitting for several portraits in his journal.

1823-4 John James Halls. Painted while Sir Peter was sheriff, altered in February 1835 to include the Lord Mayor's collar, and given to the Saddlers' Company. It was destroyed with the Saddlers' Hall in December 1940. J.J. Halls also painted portraits of Lady Laurie, John and Robert Peter Laurie.

1834 February/November. Thomas Phillips R.A. Painted in entertaining gown, collar and jewel of the Lord Mayor, It now hangs in Haddington Court House. A copy of this portrait, with legs added by Fraser in 1838, was given to Bethlehem Hospital, and now hangs in the Saddlers' Hall. A mezzotint engraved by James Scott from the portrait was published in 1839.

1836 June. John Lilley. Painted for North British Life Assurance Company.

1841 April. Sir David Wilkie R.A. A portrait in the possession of the Laurie family was exhibited at the Royal Academy. A portrait was taken from this by F. Cruickshank in January 1849 for a locket for Margaret Laurie, which was later published as a lithographic print.

1854 October. Sir Francis Grant R.A. Painted for the Union Bank, London. An engraving of this portrait was made by James Ford and published in London on 4 March 1857.

* Edward Geoffrey O'Donoghue, *Bridewell Hospital* (London 1929, pp 226-7)
† I.G. Doolittle, *The City of London and its Livery Companies* (London, 1982, p 28 and 38)
‡ George Unwin, *The Gilds and Companies of London* (London, 1908, p 345)

The Editor

Elizabeth Shepherd took an upper second B.A. in history from Westfield College, University of London, in 1982. In the following year she completed the diploma in archive administration at University College, London. In 1985 she was admitted an M.A. in archive studies by the University of London. Combining her interest in the Livery Companies of the City of London (she is a freeman and member of the Merchant Taylors' Company by Patrimony) and her training in history and archival techniques, she was able to undertake this work for the Worshipful Company of Saddlers.

THE JOURNAL

I, Peter Laurie, was born 3d March 1778 at Sandersdean in the parish of Haddington. All the information I ever could obtain respecting my ancestors is that the family of the Lauries have been respectable farmers at Stitchill near Kelso and where there names are to be found in the parish books and tombstone for two hundred years. *Although farmers, I find Major Laurie on the tombstone which suggests they must have been opulent and respectable.* I have therefore every reason to think they were a bold and heroic race as none but such lived upon the borders when the enmity so long subsisted between the Scots and English.

Pedigree

And I find the other Lauries are upon the Borders in the west Dumfreshire where Sir Robert Laurie the head of the name resides. And from all I can learn, we are of Saxon blood. My father John Laurie was born at Stitchill and married at an early age a Miss Wilson by whom he had nine children. When she died, he married my mother Agnes Thomson of a respectable family, also farmers, by whom he had two daugters and myself, who was the youngest. My father left Stitchill, went to Queenscairn, afterwards to Kedgley. How long he was in these farms I do not know, but he took possession of Sandersdean, Whit Sunday 1777. I was born in the March following of my brothers and sisters. I have but one remark to make: they had no ambition, *no choice but* to lead a humble, quiet and religious life. They have done so and, although they have not distinguished themselves in any manner, they have never done any thing dishonorable or disreputable, and although they have never become rich, they have always been respectable. Of my early days I know little, only that I was a pet being the youngest. My mother died 1784. I well recollect what was much talked about. The great fall of snow in 1784 which prevented the farmers getting home on the Friday evening. The snow was so deep the horses could not penetrate the snow wreathes[1]. My father being a heavy man did not get home until next day and this so frightened my mother in her weak state and bad health, hastened her death.

School

My father seceeded *in early life* from the Church of Scotland and I was baptized by the great John Brown of Haddington and we all had a religious education and a good example shown us by our parents. And my destination was for the Church and was for that purpose placed at the Latin school, first at Morham and then at Haddington. But my father in 1787 *married* Isabella Carfrae a woman of very respectable connexions and of suitable age. By this marriage my fate was fixed. Like most of stepmothers, she determined to make a clear house as soon as possible, and my prospects of being a minister were now at an end and Latin given up and I was destined by this women, who soon obtained an ascendancy over my father's mind, as is the case, I believe, with all second or third marriages. My brother, who was a master sadler at Jedburgh, applied for me and at 12 years of age I was sent to him.

While at school I was on good terms with the other boys. I never fought but twice. I had to go from my father's house two miles. On the half holidays I had a poney. On the other days I walked and carried my dinner with me. But the Fridays when my father came to Haddington market was a happy day. I had a pocket penny this day and always rode home behind my father on horse back and always upon the same horse *Datee* which my father rode for 15 years. And he had her buried in a field near his house with her skin on,. and it was a mournful day with us all when she, Dattee, died.

Character of my father

My father was a cheerful religious man, never missed the family worship daily in his house. We went to Haddington every Sunday and remained during morning and afternoon services – the Reverend Mr Brown frequently came to Sandersdean and, if I recollect, he was a man of much humour. I was very attached to my good and kind father who was[2] remarkable for his cheerfulness and for always having and selling good horses of his own breeding. And he was an early farmer, he always boasted of taking the lead in seedtime and harvest. My stepmother was a very bad tempered woman and one who I much disliked. Of my own mother I knew but little, but I have always heard her spoken of as a genteel well-informed woman and she died at a very early age and was buried in Morham church yard. Why my father selected Morham parish for his family graves instead of Haddington I never knew, but I suppose it was because it was nearer his own house.

Jedburgh journey

I never can forget the day I was sent to Jedburgh. I was but 12, the poney but two and not broken in, but my father, who never saw any difficulties, set me of on a winter's day with good advice. Before I got over the Lammer Moor hills a dreadful fall of snow took place. My poney was frightened, and became restive upon the top of the hill. I gave myself up for lost, but religion was so planted in my young mind, I prayed most fervently and after great obstinacy on the part of my poney and grief on my own part, a traveller came and led the poney several miles on the road, until we came to Lauder. My poney and myself were then refreshed and I went on my way rejoicing. I often reflect upon this incident, for had that traveller not come at that time I might have perished in the snow. There was no house within several miles of me.

Jedburgh

The novelty of my new situation at Jedburgh pleased me, and my brother always had a good poney or two and I had to carry things in the way of business to Merto[3]and all over the country. My family have often compared me to Joseph, and an occassion now happened which has become *one and* the most important in my life and it proves how mysterious are the ways of God to man. The best of all authorities state that the very hairs of our head are numbered and a sparrow cannot fall without his permission. My brother was harsh and severe with me and on one occasion when I had quarreled with his daughter, he beat me so unmercifully that I exhibited the wails or marks on the body so raised by a whip to a magistrate in Jedburgh and *he* ordered my brother at once to give me up my indentures. Had this not occurred, I might have remained a poor small sadler at Jedburgh as was the intention. But when released I went to an uncle, Mr Mills, Sweethope, near Stitchill, who sent a horse with me to Lauder and I walked over the hills to Sandersdean.

Edinburgh 1792

My father then took me into Edinburgh and after calling at many shops I got a *situation* with a Mr Bruce, Bristow, first, where after remaining nearly a year I got to the first shop in Edinburgh, Mr Maxton's. At Mr Bruce's I could learn nothing. I was 14 years of age when I went to Mr Maxton's and was bound *for 3 years* as an outdoor apprentice. And although I had but 4/- per week and 5/- per week for the last year, yet I was the happiest lad in the world to get into a house where there was something to learn and where I think the first and the most powerful emotions of my mind developed itself. I mean that desire of my mind to get on in the world and to distinguish myself by great attention to business and occasionally writing in my master's books I soon became so great a favourite that the apprentice above me caused his father to call upon Mr Maxton and complain of my being put over him. My mind began to expand itself during the 3 years in the shop. There were two very superior, well educated young men. They were great politicians and at that period the 'Friends of the People' began to hold meetings in Edinburgh and my youthful mind soon became imbued with these political notions. We had in the shop the 'London Morning Chronicle' and other publications. I had the good fortune to sit next Mr Roberts, who was well read, and I got hold of 'Guthries Grammar' and the notion of a globe and the manners of different nations and the history of the world, that I often sat up great part of the night poring over that most excellent book. And when any difficulty occurred I asked questions of Mr Roberts, such as the nature of the tides, trade winds etc and such was my thirst (for) knowledge I went to Mr Paton's evening school, who was celebrated for his writing and I was much improved under him. But I well recollect he was most anxious to instil into the minds of the scholars principles not at all favorable either to religion or loyalty.

Politicks

One of my fellow apprentices was in the court when Messrs Palmer, Margaret and others were tried for sedition. He unguardly applauded in the court the persons' defence and was sent to prison. Mr Maxton told us all of this and looking at me said, 'You too, you young whippersnapper, you must attend the "Friends of the People".' I confessed I had done so, would do so no longer and I kept my word. My father who had become acquainted with my own notions in favor of liberty, chiefly from my own letters to him, always came and took me out of Edinburgh on the King's birthday, as there were generally riots on that day and well knowing the enthusiasm of my mind and my fanciful and heroic ideas, he thought I might join the inconsiderate and might get into a scrape.

Drama

Finding my political career dangerous, I now took to the drama. The players used to borrow whips etc from our shop and generally gave an order or two. And never can I forget the first play I saw. It was[4] 'Othello'. I thought myself in a fairy land. I slept none the night after I witnessed this play. I bought plays, and my favourite play was 'Douglas'[5]. Like many other boys I fancied myself young Norval and continually was exclaiming to myself 'if I live not honor'd, must not live'. Many a walk I took in the meadows after the hours of business secretly studying 'Douglas'. But during all this period I was as attentive to business as if I had had no other study. The best proof I can give, that in three years I became foreman over 13 men. Partly in consequently of the removal of Mr Roberts and Mr Keadie *to London* and partly from the partiality of Mr Maxton, my theatrical studies were my secret as I constantly attended the Reverend Mr Hall and often saw my relation the Reverend Mr Aitchison, Leith. Still the reputation of Mr Henry Johnstone sent all the young men of Edinburgh mad after theatricalls.

1796

After my time had expired and I had become foreman, I might have remained long in Edinburgh but for all the men striking for the advance of wages and they pleased my vanity by asking me to be the spokesman on the occassion. Accordingly in *May 1796*, we formed a half circle in the shop and I made a speech upon the value of our time etc. My master said he would advance all but me, who he considered the ringleader. I immediately stated I should set of for London on the following Thursday and wrote to my father to get my linen ready and I should go of to London. Mrs Maxton, on the Monday morning, with whom I always was a great favourite, begged me to remain and she would make friends between Mr Maxton and myself. But I had written *to my father* and was all on fire to go to London. And I said I would get a foreman, and did get one, *to come in my place, one Anderson from another shop in Edinburgh*. And on the Thursday I set of for Sandersdean.

During my stay in Edinburgh I had from my master particularly, obtained great confidence in my own talents as a workman, and as a young man thought I was[6] destined yet to cut a figure in life. My pride was great, if I had any thing to carry I went the private ways and shunned all acquaintance that was not superior to myself, was fond of appearing well dressed, and cared little what I eat or what I drank. And upon reflection I was too rapidly raised by my master and was too much a Roman in sentiment, imbibed by the books and papers so much read at that period, and imbibed with sentiments utopion and very unfit for real life. Yet I always like to see young men have an open, generous mind, it naturally becomes cold and contracted as we become older. The only pain I felt at leaving Edinburgh was displeasing Mr Maxton who was to me one of the kindest and best of masters, who was like a father and who is in all respects a most excellent man. He had one habit which I always admired *him* for. He never wished to find his men idle, and when on the stairs he always coughed as a warning and he found us all at work when he entered. On one occasion we were all at the fire, he coughed, one fell and a dozen fell over him. Mr Maxton came in, took his hat, and walked *out*. I think that conduct made us more ashamed of ourselves than if he had scolded us for an hour.

I, who was always very susceptible of the tender passion, left two young ladies to whom I felt attached. One was a relation. But distance and other objects in London had the effect upon me that it has upon most young men, who[7] soon forget the companions of their youth. I saw very little of society, so called, *in Edinburgh*. My time was employed during the day at my business and in reading in the evening. But I well recollect I was anxious to return to Edinburgh to commence business after I had, in London, acquired a sufficient knowledge of my trade.

Set off for London

I had my dreams of greatness at that period. I quitted Edinburgh with a panting heart to see London. I arrived at my father's and probably he would have been unwillingly to part with me, but my stepmother felt no reluctance to part with me. My brother Robert on one horse and I on the other, rode to Berwick *and a young man named Nimms*. And when we arrived, the struggle for passengers was so great that I believe I might have come for[8] nothing, but I paid the fare which was bout 2 guineas. I had a few letters to friends but my spirit could not brook the idea of calling upon anyone, fearing they might think I wanted something, and although I had but a few pounds, I was determined to get work if possible before I left any letters. The sea voyage, I should have noted before, I did not like. And the Berwick smack reached the river, we all landed at Earith and walked to London, and came to an old fellow apprentice who had left Mr Maxton's sometime previous to my leaving Edinburgh.

London

I had a young man with me, a Mr Nimms. When we arrived there was no work to be had. I husbanded my little resources and shaved two or three times a day thinking a beard would make me look more like a man, as the objection was they thought me a run away apprentice as I was only 18 and looked young and delicate for my age. At last I got employment[9] at a Mr Tibbs' in the Borough, who had a smart daughter. And I had good clothes and I recollect he found my coat very neatly folded and he said, like all Scottsman, I was too fond of dress and abused me and I left his place much grieved. As I had agreed to go to Norwood with Miss Tibbs the following Sunday and I think Mr Tibbs picked this quarrel with me to prevent my going with his daughter but he was a little crazy. I got into several minor shops, but I found what was considered a very good workman in Edinburgh was but an indifferent one in London.

At Godsman to improve

And determined to be fully master of my trade and a difficult task it is to be master of that trade, I articled myself to Mr Godsman, St Martin's Street for 12 months at 10/6 *per week* to find myself in everything except lodging. And Mr Godsman who was one of the best workmen in London was to make me perfect in the business. He did so, I then went to Mr Gibson's, Coventry Street, the first house then in London and had nearly double the wages I had with Mr Godson. I had a friend at Layton, Essex, Mr Aitchison, then in good circumstances and another relation Mrs Norton in the Boro and with them I generally spent my Sundays after going to church in the morning. They were very kind to me. At Mr Gibson's there was a young man fond of theatricals and he led me to several spouting societies[10] and private theatres and I felt the same desire that I had had in Edinburgh rekindled in my breast. I first attempted a recitation and was highly applauded. I then undertook a character,[11] the lord mayor in 'Richard the 3d', little thinking at that time that I might afterwards be a real lord mayor. I went on playing thrifling characters still attending closely to my business.

Whippy's

I this year removed to Mr Whippy's where I had better work and better wages. Mr Whippy was very kind and I became a kind of collecting clerk to him. I remained about a year with him until I went to Mr Pollock as his foreman at 20 years of age. Here I was quite at home, *sometimes* dined with my master and went to church with his sons *at Orange Street chapel* and during the whole time I was with Mr Pollock I never was absent but two days and that was occasioned by my practising a tragic fall and hurt my arm.

Drama

Notwithstanding my attention to business I was closely studing the drama, thinking to make it my profession, being tired of being journeyman and seeing no prospect of being a master. When it came to my turn to choose a play at our private theatre, I selected the 'Iron Chest'[12]. Mr Morrison had Mortimer and I had Wilford. I shall not soon forget the impression I made in rehearsing Wilford, they were all astonishd. The play was well got up and my fame as a first rate private performer established. I then played Romeo, Douglas, but the character I most[13] excelled in was Fredrick in 'Lovers' Vows'[14]; and that play was so well got up that a Mr Haynes took the Richmond Theatre and we played the piece at his benifit. My favourite piece of recitation was the 'Hermit'[6] and when ever it was my night, when it was my *turn, the room was* fuller than any other night. About this time I became very intimate with the family where there were 3 daughters. One of them was as fond of playing as myself and an attachment commenced which I found very difficult to break of, yet I was not in a condition to marry. I had an excellent place. Mr Pollock had the King's business *at Charing Cross* where he resided and I had the management of the house in Piccadilly.

About the middle of 1799 my beloved father very suddenly died. The letter containing the melancholy news I never read, I only saw from the letter that my dear father was no more. I took the letter into Hyde Park where I purposed to to give vent to my grief away from the gaze of man, but I lost the letter and I was in a state of grief I cannot describe, at the death of so kind and so beloved a parent.

When I recovered my spirits, I determined to go once more and see my relations in the north, but as I had resolved to try[16] the drama as a profession I postponed going untill the ensuing spring. I had two objects in this; to try my fortune upon the stage without Mr Pollock's knowledge, and if I was unsuccessful I should still retain my situation with him. The other object was by letter to break of a connexion when I thought I could not be happy if I had married the young lady. But soon after my father's death, my brother Robert wrote and advised[17] me to call upon Mr Richards who had married my older brother's, John, daughter, and offer him £100 for the lease of Sandersdean to be given to[18] his wife's brother, a boy under his care, who was, by the laws of Scotland, entitled to the lease, as the leases in Scotland were considered the same as freehold. I completed the arrangement with Mr Richards and gave satisfaction to all parties. Such was the independence of my mind, although I knew Mr Richards was married to my neice, her father having died before I came to London, I never called thinking it might be supposed I wanted something. But after this I found Mr Richards the kindest of friends and I dined with him and Mrs Richards every Sunday.

About this period several young men clerks got up a dancing assembly. I was one of (the) number, but I soon found dancing was not to my taste. I had at

Jedburgh gone to the dancing school but never was fond of it. I never was very fond of music and always dreaded sitting up late in the evening and I can say dancing, card playing and drinking was always avoided by me all my life. We soon began[19] a private debating society, which lasted only a few months, this I liked much better. The assembly and the debating society and also the 'Muses Voteries', the house where we had song and recitation, was all soon given up but I continued perseverlingly studying the drama, all this unknown to Mr Pollock. But I recollect he had us all to sup with him Christmas 1799. I was engaged to play 'Douglas' and got away, played my part, and joined the others at supper at 10 o'clock. And after supper Mr John Pollock, then a little boy, spoke the speech 'my name is Norval etc'. I thought I was then discovered, but it was not so. I continued to go to church with Mr Pollock's sons. They were all very clever young men and I learnt much from them in conversation. And a more honorable upright man than Mr Pollock I never knew, and all his family partake of their honorable father's good qualities.

In February 1800 I sailed for Scotland determined to try the Edinburgh stage. Stephen Kemble's company was then in Edinburgh. I had letters from London to Mr Buchan, a writer in Edinburgh, who introduced me to Mr Henry Siddons who was managing the company. Mr Kemble was at York or Newcastle. I wished to play 'Douglas' but they had no Lady Randolf and at last 'Lovers' Vows' was advertised and Fredrick 'by a young gentleman, being his first appearance'. All this time I was living amongst and calling upon my friends. I had previously gone to my brother at Sandersdean. And all was settled either to go of to London if unsuccessful or to take an engagement if I got favourable terms. I went in the theatre by the name of Buchan. I made my appearance and was so well received that Mr Siddons announced *that* the play would be repeated on the Saturday I had played on the Wednesday. I was so encouraged by my reception that I told many of my friends, and they came on the Saturday. And I also tried Walter in the 'Children of the Wood'[20]. I was equally successful in Fredrick, but did not make a hit in Walter. I had never played the part in private. Mr Siddons offered me the best salary to play the young tragic parts and to have 4 benefits. And this I would, and at first did, agree to, but my friends interfered and perswaded me that an actor would disgrace the family. And I declined the engagement, went again to East Lothian, and came to Berwick and saild for London. And I suffered so much from sea sickness being eight days at sea, that I have never got reconciled to the smell of a ship since and I believe no one ever suffered so much as I did on that occasion.

While in Edinburgh I wrote to the young lady and made every excuse I could for not entering into the holy state of wedlock but all in vain. The young lady wrote what ever were my fortunes she would share my good or bad fortune with me. This matter pressed more upon my mind than any thing that had occurred. I was but young, but because young I had promised and had I kept my[21] promise I might have been *at this day an* actor, which would have been a great misfortune *to me and all my friends*. When I came back Mr Pollock was very glad to see me return and I went on still studying the drama.

West Indies

But closely attending to learning I forgot to mention that two years after I came to London I had an offer to go to the West Indies to follow my business. But fortunately I was advised to ask higher terms than was given and another young man[22] was satisfied with less terms[23] than I required. Thus I was fortunately prevented going to that grave of our countrymen, the West Indies. I had also at one time a great desire to go to New York and seek my fortune in America.

1800

But I became so fond of London after 3 years' residence that I was very anxious to remain. I was much vexed at paying a visit with the young lady I was courting to find that the party on the Sunday evening[24] began singing songs. The religious impression of my youth rose in me and I never forget what I consider'd the most sinful *Sunday* evening in my *life*. After I had fairly, but I freely confess not so honorably as I could wish, released myself from my promise, all parties consenting, and the young lady leaving England for India where she married well, and her husband soon dying, she married a[25] second husband and this has ever been a great consolation to me. I believe it was the only promise I ever made which I broke and this has often given me great pain, yet it has been a pleasing reflection that the young lady married a British officer and she could therefore not be disappointed.

But being always very susceptible of the tender passion, another very beautiful young lady[26] soon attracted my attention. She daily passed Mr Pollock's with a very old lady and a footman. And as I had studied the drama and studied mankind I understood the language of the eye and was romantic enough to suppose I had made as great an impression on the young lady's heart as she had done on mine. I went to all the chapels about Brompton and at last I found her at Brompton chapel. I am afraid the lesson, the powerful sermon of Mr Harrison the preacher, made but little impression on me the first day I discovered this beautiful lady in his chapel. I took care that she should see me and that her aunt, the old lady, should not. I went every Sunday for some time to this chapel. I could not see her by herself and I durst not write fearing my letters might get into other hands and displease her friends. I employed a clever workman in Mr Pollock's shop to follow the footman and enter into conversation with him. He found him reading a label or petition hung on the breast of a blind beggar, who became the subject of the conversation. It ended in the two having a pot of beer at the first alehouse and I learnt all the particulars of her family etc. I wrote a letter with the intention of giving it to her the first opportunity. This was soon afforded, for there was a review of volunteers in Hyde Park[27]. All London seemed to be there and amongst the throng I saw the young lady and her aunt.

There was much difficulty in getting out at Hyde Park Corner the crowd was so great. I kept near the young lady and assisted her and her aunt through the crowd. The young lady privately took my letter and the old lady thanked (me) as a stranger. I saw her a few days after and walked nearly a mile into town with her but unfortunately I met Mrs Pollock who was astonished to see me walking with a lady and a footman, stopt me and questioned me to my great mortification if such and such orders had been completed. I met her again and delivered a letter privately as before passing a crowd in the street and I remember two gentlemen observed me and said I was a clever fellow. I promised to meet her but business interfered. I found I was not in a condition to marry, she left Brompton, and I never saw her afterwards but once, walking over the London docks in the following summer and we cast many a long, long look at each other. I pointed her out to Mr and Mrs Richards who admired her beauty and figure. Miss Bunyan's brother is manager of the Norwich Union, is a member of the Saddlers' Company and excellent person. I once asked about his sister. She married a clergyman and resides in Devonshire and has a large family.

The time was now approaching when I was to decide on my future life. Mr Pollock's son had now become old enough to be the foreman or master and I had been so long master that it was unpleasant to submit to those I had instructed. And having no capital and being unwilling to lay myself under obligation to any one I again thought of the stage. And in the first floor of Mr Pollock's lodged a Mrs and Miss Gunning and having heard of my fame as a private actor they[28] spoke to their particular friend Miss Jane Porter who is distinguished for her popular 'Travels of Wallace' etc etc[29]. She wrote to Mr Tate Wilkinson at York and refered him to my performance at Edinburgh. Mr Wilkinson wrote to Mr H. Siddons and *then* wrote to Miss Porter and I had performed Fredrick in 'Lovers' Vows' with much promise, Walter in the 'Children in the Wood' quite the reverse, these words were too important for me ever to forget them, that Mr Thorn was quiting his company and I was to come and take the field in the first line and that he had advertised me for 'Romeo' on a certain day giving me time to reach York, that I should have the first salary and 4 benefits in the year. Mr Aitchison my friend by chance called and I showed him the letter. He went immediately to Mr Richards. They came together and Mr Richards said if I could relinquish the stage he would assist me in getting into business and that if I didnot succeed in business I could but then go upon the stage as I was young enough. This proposition pleased[30] me and I wrote to Mr Wilkinson that my friends would not let me go upon the stage.

1801

This was about the end of 1800 and I resolved to try my good fortune in trade. And I was several months looking out for a house or shop where the coming in would be but trifling. And an old fellow apprentice who had begun in Duke Street, Grosvenor Square offered me a share of his business, but we could not agree about who's name should have first in the firm. And at last I saw a small house in Oxford Street. The bill was put on the window on the Saturday, I mentioned it to Mr Richards on the Sunday, and on the Monday I went to the landlord near Edgeware and agreed to give all he asked, £50 a year. We had no sooner signed[31] a memorandum, than another person came in and offered £60. But the landlord was honourable and I took possession. And in the 1st April 1801 I opened my small shop and as I then took my leave of theatricals for ever, I shall only remark no young man should study the drama with the intention of performing, no man should join any private theatre unless he has firm fixed religious principles and one of firm resolution.

During the 3 years I played occasionally in private *I* never made even a common acquaintance of any person connexted with the company. I was civil to all, never called upon any of them nor did they call upon me. I, through life, endavored to excell in what I undertook. I understood my business well. I could play Romeo, Douglas, Wilford, Fredrick, Octavian and other characters to the satifaction[32] of myself and the approbation of my friends but it was remarkable although I was generally cheerful I could do nothing comic. I have given a proof of this when I mention my failure in Walter. The more pathetic the more I was successful. And upon the whole I have no hesitation in saying I was much benifited by my studies. I was always sober, disliked cards, late hours, dancing and above all singing clubs but the greatest merit I had was I knew when to stop. I resolved after I began business never to tread the stage unless I was unsuccessful in trade.

I wish I could add that my brother and sister actors and actresses *at the private theatres* had known when to stop. They, at least the most part of them, became so fond of the profession that they went into the country and I have forgotten them all except one or two who have been very unfortunate and have applied to me for relief. It is a dangerous amusement for young men and certain destruction to females. This I think is generally the case, yet there may be exceptions, I however confess I know but few. When I say I benefited by it, I mean it gave me an ease in expressing myself and gave me a facility in language and made me, from study, get rid of my Scotch, and in after life it gave me the power of addressing public meetings and also gave me a knowledge of my own voice and feattures. At that thime there was no mechanic's institute or society for science within my reach, otherwise I think I should have improved my mind more by attending to arts and sciences than the drama. I recollect only one private actor who was successful in trade, that is Mr Mivart who keeps the largest hotel in London, 'Mivart's Hotel', Brook Street, who is living and is prosperous.

Business

On the 1st April 1801 I began business. I had my little shop fitted up as neat and at as little expense as possible as I always dreaded getting into debt. I called and gave my orders to various wholesale tradesmen and refered them to Mr Richards who used to make him answerable for me to a certain amount, but so good an opinion had they of me that only two called upon Mr Richards. I can conceive no time so important in a man's life as when he begins business. I had very little connexion and of those I calculated upon, very few became customers. I knew I excelled in one part of my business, making ladies saddles. I advertised them upon an improved principle. I got up very early and worked very late, lived as moderately as possible, and I never can forget, in fact no one but those who begin business can understand, the feeling of a young man anxious[33] to get forward, when he succeeds. My business began with great promise, I soon got a journeyman. I was astonished at my own success, and by the middle of the summer I had a tolerable business and had begun to get a few customers of the first rank. I forgot all theatricals and politics and now thought of nothing but being a first rate tradesman.

My prospects were so bright that I now thought of looking out for a wife and I went a round of all the church's and chapels. To have a gay and an amusing lady[34] as a companion and friend is delightful, but to choose a wife is very difficult. Then we want family connextion, his for life, a good housewife, an exemplary mother should there be any children, is required and when a man wishes to be respectable in life he considers the relations of the wife that is to be. All these matters pressed themselves on my mind and this was my Sunday's study, the week days, I had almost said night and day, was devoted to increasing my business. I had heard of young tradesmen putting out packing cases in the morning and taking them in in the evening to make a shew of business if they had it not. This was not my case, but I made a good shew of *the* business I had, nay, I would keep the windows open[35] till 10 and 11 at night that we might be seen working, and I soon obtained the character of an industrious young man. I do not recollect any thing particular during 1801, but at the close of that year when I balanced my books I was delighted beyond all bounds at my success, and as my landlord offered me a lease if successful, I had my lease for 21 years.

1802

After all my anxious enquiries and going to all the churches, I found in Swallow Street a young lady, her father a most respectable and[36] worthy man and an elder of the church. My study of the drama learned me to 'use mine eyes' and by constantly attending the church I soon, I thought, had made myself observed. And on the 14 February 1802 I sent a Valentine, the poetry was my own, not good but expressive of my situation, and this I sent being almost certain the writer would be known, and it was so. Still I went on pursuing my successful career, making no aquaintances, spending very little, and what is remarkable although I began *almost* without a shilling I never found myself inconvenienced for want of money.

At last I resolved to make my honorable intentions known to Mr Jack, the father of the young lady. I wrote to him and knowing I should not (be) getting a written answer I said I would call upon a certain evening for a reply, begging earnestly that I might have permission to visit the family. After taking a glass of brandy and water to keep my courage up and set of for Hans Place, Mr Jack's residence and after a great deal of throbbing at my heart, anxious for the interview yet dreading a repulse, at last I plucked up resolution to knock at the door.

I was admitted and was[37] received in a very friendly *way*, but was told by Mr Jack his three daughters were upon a visit from home and that they would not be at home for a day or two. This was a very prudent step. I then unfolded my tale, mentioned my attachment, my success, the certainty of making a fortune etc, and he very kindly advised me to go on for another year or two and then to come back but on no account to think any more of the matter, then that his daughter Margaret, the middle one, was not 18, and that I must think no more about it. But this advice only increased my ardour and I never failed to go to church and sighed and looked, sighed and looked and made an impression. And as they attended a prayer meeting and I was always anxious to have a religious wife, and a woman loses half her value when she is not pious, I attended and attempted to walk home with her. She willingly took my arm but Dr Nicol came up snatched her from me, said the young lady was under his care and that I had come with very improper motives to church. I said nothing then but after the Reverend gentleman had got home my feelings and pride was so roused that I called upon Dr Nicol and demanded an explanation which he willingly gave me and we parted friends[38].

Mrs Trotter, wife of Dr Trotter joint minister of Swallow Street, found me out, invited me to her house and she was so pleased with me[39] that she had the Misses Jacks and some other friends *to tea*. I saw Miss Margaret home but was again told by her father he would not permit me to have anything to do with him or his family, but I found Mrs Jack was my friend. I sent the statement of my affairs, perservered, ultimately got permission to visit the family, and after much opposition on the part of Mr Jack and much support and encouragement from Mrs Jack, Dr and Mrs Trotter, I got the consent of all parties. But Mr Jack very justly objected to my small house and most generously offered to assist me in getting another house, for which purpose I got fortunately a house a very short distance from my old one and a corner house.

And on the 6 January 1803 I married this Margaret Jack in St Martin's church, the wedding dinner was at the Ship in Greenwich, there were present Dr and Mrs Trotter, Mr and Mrs Richards and Mr Fraser, and[40] returned home to Oxford Street. I gratefully remark that Mr Jack 3 *months* before my marriage placed £500 in my banker's hands in my name. This was very generous, but I did not draw a shilling and after I was married he gave me a further sum, stateing that at his death all his daughters should be[42] made equal in their fortune. He did not settle any sum upon his daughter, always observing that if you entrusted any one with your child you may without fear trust him with her fortune. I do not altogether subscribe to this in a commercial country like England where property so often changes hands it may be as well to secure an independence on the daughter when there is fortune sufficient.

I recollect nothing important during 1803 except the famous Bill of Lord Sidmouth's for making every man a soldier. I became a volunteer in my parish corps, and had the good fortune to be selected for the light infantry. After all men enrolled amounting to 6 or 700 we assembled in the court yard, Devonshire House. When a ring was made and all the recruits were marched singly, the very awkward were sent into the battalion, the tallest went to the grenadiers and the best looking were honoured with the green feathers and this was consider'd much greater honor and distinction than to be made a non-commissioned officer. And no one was considered elligable for a commissioned officer but a man out of business.

I was placed upon the committee, this suited my taste better than marching and drilling in Hyde Park. I much disliked soldiering but as I never failed to avail myself of anything that would increase my business and reputation. We had[42] circulars desiring us to get our belts, *accoutrements* from a house in town at 27/6 a set. I went about a set for myself, the person to whom I applied said he could supply the whole regiment for 25/- and allow me a handsome profit. I had interest sufficient with the committee to call in the circulars and issue fresh ones recommending the volunteers to get their belts from me and I got a good many customers and made something satisfactory by this fortunate affair.

1804

I was soon compelled to serve the office of constable and as I always prefered the civil to the military office I retired from the army and connected myself with the civil power. I was thus enabled, which was my chief object, to devote my time to the increase of my business, which was increasing beyond my most sanguine, and they were sanguine, expectations. About this time I sent to Scotland for a[43] son of my sister Agnes, whom I put to school, and he there went and has ever continued to be called Laurie although his father's name was Snaddon but as I conceived he had not behaved properly to my sister I had a dislike to his name and never allowed my nephew to be called Snaddon. And I got not only John but his brother Robert, *mentioned afterwards* who came afterwards to dezire their names changed by the King to Laurie and in this succeeded when I was sheriff, 1824.

During 1805 nothing remarkable occurred. Dr Nicol who had been averse to our marriage from the purest of motives now became my most intimate and we all went on very happily together. 1806 and 1807 passed in the same manner.

1808

My business still increasing, but in 1808 I heard a large contract was out for military saddley, I had not been written to. It was[44] for the East India

Company. The moment I heard of it I went to Mr John Moser who had lately returned from India, he was kind and anxious to serve me, gave me a letter to Sir Thomas Metclalf who desired me to look at the patterns at the military warehouses and send a tender. I did so and succeeded, but those who had been used to have these contracts reported I was not a military contractor and that I was unable to fulfil the contract. Mr James Cunningham, the inspector, came and saw what I was doing, had confidence I sent my goods. The disappointed contractors again wrote *in* all sorts of complaints against my articles. Mr Innes an honest and independent director said this might be jealousy and an endeavor to crush a young successful man who had roused their envy and very properly called in Mr Birnie, now Sir Richard, who[45] had retired *from business* and could not be interested. I had never known Mr Birnie but he said nothing could be better than the stores I had supplied, and I continued for five or six years.

I received the third of the orders, the other two thirds were given to my old master Mr Pollock and Mr Reaton partner with Samuel Jackson, the rich carrier and I made more money by the East India Company than I did by anything I ever touched. I recollect on one occassion I received £7,000. I knew no broker, but well knew by reputation the house of Antrobus and Co. and they purchased in 1811 or 1812 Exchequer bills, as I was not sure lest I should need the money again and the first money I ever funded was 1000 India Stock, 11 May 1813. And ever since that period I have been annually adding to my funded property.

But in 1813 the governor general, Mr Hastings wrote home for 700 sets of cavalry appointments but by some mistake in the indent it was 7000, I knew for 8000 cavalry it was impossible that so much a quantity should be wanted. I wrote in to the directors but in vain, they said they must supply the 7000. The quantity being so large they were advertised and Mr Jackson the carrier got the contract at a mere trifle lower than my low estimate and I never from that period got any thing from the company but to make patterns etc etc. I was however, ever grateful for my past favor.

1809

In 1809 my wife, who had always been in a very delicate state of health was recommended to go by sea to Scotland for her health. She did so and was away 5 months, when she very much recovered and returned in October with Miss Fortune Aitchison her friend and companion, and has often said she spent her days in Scotland very delightfully and all my friends were very attentive, more so than I was, for my attention to business had become so incessent and indespensible, so much of it resting on my own shoulders, that I could not spare time to go to Scotland.

While she was there my brother[46] Alexander, who had lost his wife a few[47] months before, brought his child 11 months old named Peter after me. The child took her fancy, partly perhaps because he was named after me. However when he was 2 years of age Mr James Thomson a relation of mine brought him to

London and he became the constant companion of my wife, and his playful society did much in restoring her health, and supplied the want of children to us both. I was quite delighted to hear a child 2 years of age speak the language of my youth, for we were both born in East Lothian and I had then been from Scotland 13 years. In 1811 my sister Agnes became again deserted by her profligate husband, and I agreed to take *her* other son Peter and farther agreed to give her a suitable maintence provided she *separated* ever *after* apart from her husband. Peter came to London, but as my[48] nephew Peter had for two years occupied the field and known by all our friends as little Peter, I called the second Robert Peter. He was then about 8 years of age and I put him to school.

1810. Four in Hand Club

At this time a new fashion arose of gentlemen driving four in hand and they enrolled themselves under the name of the 'Four in Hand Club'. Several of my customers became members, Mr Buxton became president. That was also an anxious time to me. Lord Say and Sele ordered a four in hand harness from one of the oldeste houses in town. Mr Humphrey Batlie ordered a four in hand harness from me. Mr Buxton superintended both and said whoever made the best should make his, I knew making his must establish him. I succeeded, and Mr Buxton ever after was my very best friend and the only return I ever could make him was, when sheriff, when I was teased by all the brewers to give them the orders for the beer for Newgate. I went to Mr Buxton and in the best way I could offered it as a small tribute of gratitude to his nephew. By getting Mr Buxton's order I secured nearly the whole of the club.

Finding I knew all the names of the members and all the movements of the club, the fashionable reporter of the 'Morning Post' called got the information which emblazoned the columns of that fashionable paper for 4 or 5 years while the club lasted. It ought to have lasted for ever, as it was a manly, noble exercise, improved the breed of horses, set the fashions for carriages and harness, but the expense was so great that very few could keep it up. Amongst the finest eights that ever was seen was the first day of the club each year. Nearly 70 carriages and four, beautiful horses, new carriages, liveries, the fashionable world in open carriages in Cavendish Square, the windows crowded with British beauty, and the club driving twice round that large square then up Oxford Street and through Hyde Park to Salthill, the park and Oxford Street crowded with the best company. The club did great good to me and[49] did harm to no one.

Nothing occurred during 1811 and 1812 that I recollect only we used to go to Brighton for a month or two in the summer. Mr Jack's family always went, Mrs Laurie remained with them and I went generally on the Saturdays and returned on the Mondays. But I am now coming to one of the (most important) years in my life.

1813

In 6 May 1813, Mrs Jack, my wife's mother, died. She was one of the kindest most generous women that ever lived and I was I believe a great favourite with her. Her death was a great loss to us all. She had never been very strong but still her death was very unexpected. She lived a religious vertuous life and I have no doubt but what was felt so keenly by us was fair to her. Not only her near relations but the poor and her acquaintances met with a severe loss.

1813 was also a very important year to me in[50] another respect. The government advertised for cavalry equipments, 4000 set. I tendered and got them at a few shillings under Maberly. I had no sooner obtained this contract than Mr Herries sent for me, he was commissary in chief, and said 10,000 additional was wanting and the whole 14,000 must be had in 6 weeks and advised me to give them up and Maberly would undertake what would ruin any other man. I said it would not ruin me, I had made such contracts and was bound by them. He gave me the 14,000. Maberly, who calculated upon my being unable, through his endeavor to ruin me and all others who opposed him sent to Birmingham and every quarter, and bought up materials to prevent my completing my contract then he could have got the order upon his own terms. But I fortunately had made sub contracts and I gave in two bondsmen of £20,000 each, viz. John Jack, my father in law, and Hugh Richard who married my niece.

I believe no man ever had more on his hands than I had then. It was in the summer season when I had all other regular business to attend to, we had to work night and day. My friends were afraid that it would be too much for my health, advised me to sleep at Hampstead to take, in some measure, the anxiety from my mind. I left London late and came to town early and to increase my anxious cares I was deceived by a sub contractor who had sent me bits if stirrups of cast instead of wrought[51] iron and Maberly, who was upon the watch, had intimation of this from Birmingham. A trial took place before the commissary general and the whole of the bits of stirrups were rejected and I should have been ruined but providentially I had in my sub contract inserted wrought iron and the contractors very properly came from Birmingham and made an oath to that effect. This I had printed and circulated and this removed all censure from me but it caused great delay. I was obliged to discontinue, by the structions of the commissary in chief, employed the sub contractors Messers Bright and Martin and got the articles from Messers Adams and Sons.

My activity and good fortune overcame all difficulties and I had nearly completed my contract. I had sent in 13,000 sets and a counter order took place as an armstice had taken place. But I was greatly vexed at Mr Herries' giving to Mr Maberly an order for 6,000 sets for the Dutch cavalry without competition and thus enabled that man to work up the very articles and materials which he had bought up for the express purpose of preventing my completing my contract and throwing it into his hands and I learnt also that he had received this order at a much higher price than I had contracted for. I wrote to Mr Herries and strongly expressed my feelings on the subject and he told me I might work up all my materials, and I made 600 additional sets and all this in 6 weeks.

Those only who know the difficulties of such contracts will sufficiently be able (to) appreciate my exertions. I afterwards returned from Hampstead but the 2 months unequalled exertions had done my health so much injury that I never would have undertaken so great task again. I had long been used to have my share of my East India contracts, but from an error they were lost to me this year and never more to return. The indents from India said 7000 equipments were required. I knew this must be a mistake, the 700 was meant. I saw the indent[52] and it was 7000 in writing. The quantity was so large the directors advertised and I lost the contract and 2000 were afterwards added making 9000 for 8000 cavalry at Bengal. After the stores were needed the error was discovered and the 9000 lasted 9 years and were all moth eaten and ruined before they left the warehouses in London.

I then looked to the British cavalry and soon got the 24 Light Dragoons, 7 Hussars and soon established my name as a military saddler under the patronage of General Sir Hussey Vivian, then Colonel Vivian, commanding the 7 Hussars. My private business continued to increase and I went on in the full career of prosperity. In the autumn we all went to Cheltenham partly for our health and partly to recover our spirits after our great loss occasioned by the death of Mrs Jack and we all returned in improved health and spirits.

1814

I have no recollection of anything occurring worth notice in 1814. I was prosperous in living, had a good share of health and increasing in fortune. In September I went with John Brownley to Paris, and a most pleasant trip it was. It was before any of Bounoparte's trophies had been removed from Paris. The contrast of the English with the French costume was so great at that time as *to* make us suppose when we landed at Calais that instead of only coming to a neighbouring nation, 21 miles distant, that we had got into another world where there was a different race of mortals. We were only 14 days away from London, 7 of which number we were in Paris. And with the assistance of an excellent valet de place and a cabriolet constantly in use we saw all that was worth seeing in Paris and was twice at Versailles. There was only one drawback upon my pleasure, the dreadful suffering I had in crossing from Dover to Calais and on returning. Mr Brownley, who is an excellent sailor, came back by Diepe and Brighton but being the longest sit I returned as I went, and I was glad to see once more the white cliffs of Dover. My wife had been at Margate for some time and returned to keep house during my trip to France. We had no other tour this year.

1815

Nothing happened during this year but the bustle of a still increasing business. We had our usual two months in the country but whether at Brighton or Cheltenham I do not recollect. But this year, from taking a very active part in various charitable institutions and generally speaking at the anniversaries I became known as rather a public man and in consequence of the death of Dr Young I was elected secretary to the 'Society in Scotland for Propagating Christian Knowledge' and Mr Thomson joint or under secretary and this year we had a large company at our annual dinner and everything went off with great eclat.

And I then became[53] acquainted with the Dukes of Kent and Sussex. I often met these princes at the numerous charitable institutions in London and much time and much money I spent in attending these dinners particularly the Scotch and yet I never had any greater partiality for the Scotch than the English, I always loved and do now most sincerely love the English. They have been ever generous and kind to me and they have enabled me to make my fortune.

1816

I have no recollection of any matter of importance occuring to me this year. I continued as prosperous as before and did not relax in my industrious habits, nor did I increase my expenditure looking forward to the day when I should reap the fruits of my unwearied exertions. And the only history I could give this year would be to refer to my day book and ledger, and purchased 2000 in the India stocks and £2715 in the navy 5 per cents, I sold out 26 July, to enable me to complete my purchase of India stock.

1817

This year was like the preceeding years employed in increasing my trade and increasing my funded property and the only occurrance this year was my going to Scotland on the 13 August and returning on the 11 September. Having suffered so much from going to sea I went the whole of the way by land, the outside of the coaches and slept at Stamford, Doncaster, York, Newcastle etc. I put up at one of the hotels in Princes's Street, Edinburgh and never did any man returning to his native country pant for morning, for we arrived late at night, more anxiously than I did, that I might see the place where I had spent the four most important years of my youth. I hired a gig and took a brother-in-law, Mr Robertson with me to East Lothian. When I saw all my friends, which was to me most gratifying, they were all glad to see me. I had assisted some of them in their less properous times than my own. This increased their joy and in many instances tears instead of words spoke our recollection of each other. It is only those who have been 17 years from their relations and returning in good circumstances able to assist and assisting that can enter into feelings I then enjoyed.

After making all my friends as happy as it was in my power to make them, I left Edinburgh for Glasgow. Being treasurer to the 'Highland School Society' I took the stage to Helingsbury[54] and then a post chaise to Luss, which was not only the nearest station in the Highlands but Dr Stuart, the most important of all the societies' friends, as he was then translating the English Bible into Gaelic. I dined with him and his most interesting and highly renowed lady, renowed not more for urbanity of manners than for his superior knowledge. I returned and slept at Hellinsbury and had, I never can forget, the coarsest sheets I ever saw. I soon took them of and slept in my own clothes and had not the best opinion of the Highlands, except of the boys who were in a station near Luss called together by the schoolmaster and explained before me, which cost sundry pieces of silver; all this tour was at my own expence.

I was greatly disappointed with Glasgow, it fell far short of my expectations. I spend an evening with Dr Chalmers which in some measure repaid me for my journey. I also saw the falls of the Clyde. And returned to London by Liverpool, Manchester and Nottingham etc, much pleased with my tour and resolved to repeat my journey as often as convenient, and I believe my relations will not soon forget my trip. This was a very wet summer and my friends remarked that the only two *or three* fair days were the two days I was in the east country. My friends upon the whole did not appear so old as I expected to find them, their cares are few, their minds easy. I had had more care and more anxiety than them all put together and my appearance doubtless told them so.

This year as in all former years, I was from London to *meet* Mr Jack's family but whether at Brighton or Cheltenham I do not recollect, but on my return I left London with Mrs Laurie who had been left in London during my Scots trip.

1818

This year was spent as the two or three preceding years, but Mrs Laurie was not very strong and I took a cottage at Turnham Green from 1 April to 1 September but quitted it in July to go to a watering place. This year I had the misfortune to lose a mare which I had ridden 7 years and had much difficulty in getting one to suit me. One I had purchased I was riding at Ealing very fast and had a dreadful fall which cut my face very much and ruined the horse's knees. At last I purchased a brown horse[55] 'Tom' which I rode for eight years. And this year I had to pay £21 for a substitute for the militia, which I thought hard having been a volunteer. I do not recollect any thing of importance this year only that I was beginning to relax a little of my exertions in Oxford Street and to throw more of the burden *of business* on John and Robert Peter Laurie and I found them both very attentive and useful. John's apprenticeship termined this year and I gave him £100 a year, bed and board until I took him into partnership. This year there was a general election and for the first time I publickly appeared in politicks having become an active member of Sir S. Romilly's committee and chairman in my parish.

1819

Took John Laurie into partnership 1 January 1819. I recollect of nothing worth mentioning this year, my business was still going on as I could wish and I no doubt took a trip as usual into the country in the autumn. I became secretary of the 'Society for Propagating Christain Knowledge' in 1815 and now became treasurer. And this year there was a very great opposition to the water companies, and I was elected treasurer and chairman of the committee for St George's parish, and here I had an opportunity of judging of public men. Many, many who joined us at first went over to the companies and only Mr Hume[56] and a few others remained steady. All the money collection was disbursed and I had a vote of thanks as treasurer. I was thus every day becoming more and more a public man and throwing the details of my business upon my partner.

1820

On the first of January this year I took my nephew John into partnership giving him a small share but I still continued to attend closely but not *quite* so assiduously as heretofore as I wished John to speak to and obtain the confidence of the customers. This year, I believe, was as fortunate for me in business as the former years but we were kept in a very agitated state in consequence of the Queen's arrival. Thro the interest of Mr Brougham we had to fit her out with every[57] article of harness etc and was paid by the Treasury.

As I did not wish to mix myself up the violent contending parties and wishing to take Mrs Laurie to Scotland I embraced this opportunity. Mrs Laurie, Peter then about 11 years old, and myself started in the summmer *by* the coach to Stamford where we slept and on the next day we joined a Mr Caley in a post chaise and went through the Dukery as it is called, a beautiful road passing the Duke of Newcastles etc, and we slept at Doncaster. We stoped a day at York, saw the interesting lunatic asylum called the Retreat, and all that was worth seeing at York and we reached Newcastle on a Saturday and remained there according to our custom not to travel on the Sunday. We on the Monday got as far as Coldstream where we slept. Then slept the following day at Kelso and was much pleased with our tour. At a small inn on the road from London to Edinburgh we called for a bottle of ale and bread and cheese. When I asked what was to pay the reply was new and astonishing to me. The clean landlady said, 'The ale is sixpence but I charge nothing for the bread and cheese.'

We took up our abode at Macgregor's Hotel but soon removed to private lodgings in St Andrew's Street. I hired a gig and we went and saw all our friends in East Lothian and with good humour and a little money to those we thought needed it, we made them all very happy. We left Peter with his father and sister for a short time, which made them all delighted. A Mr and Mrs Martin had promised in London to meet us in Edinburgh, they did so, and after remaining 14 days in Edinburgh dining out every day, receiving the greatest hospitality, visiting Roslin and all the attractions about Edinburgh, we hired an open barouch and set of for Perth, our party consisting of 5, with a very droll coachman John Clerk who took us by Kinross where we dined, called and saw the rector, Pithcathley. And knocked up one of the horses when we reached Perth, after bleeding and doing all we could we could not get the horse to move in the morning and as Clerk was engaged to take us to Glasgow he was obliged to hire another horse at Perth.

We were delighted with Perth, proceeded to[58] Dunkeld up the Tay to Dalncaley and Inverary to Luss and Glasgow going about the rate of 20 miles a day. The beds were miserable but Martin was droll, Mrs Martin in good humour with all she saw or heard, so that the time passed away very pleasently. At Anochar we heard a Gaelic sermon to a sleepy Highland congregation. We were sometime in Glasgow, went to Lanark, Queens, Sterling etc. And returned home by Dumfries, Manchester, Derby, Nottingham etc and had a very pleasant tour. Resolved to go very soon again to Scotland. Thought the Highlanders very plain, particularly the women, but very civil and obliging. Still I thought there was no place like old England. We were (away) about 10 weeks.

I recollect nothing further this (year) but this; the kindness of the Lord Mayor Thorpe. I had the pleasure of witnessing for the first time the lord mayor's grand entertainment[59], 9th November, little thinking at that time I should in all probability hold the offices of sheriff and alderman and perhaps chief magistrate, and this being at the time of the Queen's trial there was more than the usual number of the nobility in town which added greatly to the effect of the dinner. And with my usual luck I got upon the hustings the chosen seats, but the reason why I got upon the hustings was I was passed for an M.P., and walked around the hall arm in arm with Lord Duncannon.

1821

I have no recollection of anything occuring this year except this, Mr Burton began Cornwall Terrace in the Regent's Park and I thought it a most desirable residence and I purchased on of the houses before it was even built up to the first floor. This year I attended constantly to business and had our usual trip in the country but when I do not recollect.

1822

This year like the last was employed in attending to business and finishing my house in Cornwall Terrace. Business still continuing very productive. We took a longer holiday at Cheltenham this year than usual and this year I attended to a great number of public charities and was appointed vice-president, treasurer etc etc. Mr Traing having come up to supply the Caledonian church this year, I was like many others attracted by these talents and joined his friends and elders for the purpose of bringing him to London and devoted much time, many evening meetings. At last we got him to London and for when a new church was erected, but as the committee were disposed to lay out more money that I thought it prudent to do, I in the following year paid my £125 and withdrew from all management having been previously one of the treasurers. A resolution which I have since proved to be a very prudent one.

On the 17 March this year died one of the best of men I ever knew, my wife's respected and beloved father. The following is upon the tomb stone in Bunhill fields written by myself and corrected by the great and good Dr Waugh D.D.

'In Memory of the above John Jack, who died on the 17 March 1822 in the 84 year of age. Educated under the pious care of his father a minister of the Church of Scotland, he illustrated during a long and *useful* life the influence of the sacred principles with which in youth his mind had been richly furnished, and preserved a reputation for eminent piety, active benevolence and conciliatiating disposition, adorned with such modesty as would have kept in the shade any worth less distinguished than his own.

To keep up the remembrance of such worth for the imitation of others, and in grateful return for the inestimable benefits of paternal tenderness and care, this stone has been raised by the hand of filial affection to the honor of the best of fathers.'

This worthy gentleman had long been the chief support of Swallow Street, best of all the other Scots churches. I had been son-in-law nearly 20 years and during the whole period there never was the slighest misunderstanding, not for one moment, a more uniform attachment could not have been than between us. He was pious without being gloomy or uncharitable. In my opinion it was impossible to find a better man. I never knew so good a man and no one could have better opportunities of forming an opinion than I[60] myself. In the summer we all spent a few months at Cheltenham, Malvern etc.

1823

This was one of the most important years in my life. In preparing to leave Oxford Street I took Robert Peter Laurie as a partner with a small share, desirous of promoting his interest and that he might be known to the numerous customers, and I agreed that the business in future was to be carried on in the names of 'John and Robert Laurie'. Having made all these arrangements and my house in Cornwall (Terrace) being finished and furnished, on my birthday 3d of March, I removed and not without regret *from* a house where I had been remarkably successful, to that which I had often desired, to look on green fields and yet be near business. Finding that all my old friends and customers often put off their orders until I was at home or they desired me to call upon them, this did not answer my purpose, which was that my two nephews should obtain the confidence of the customers, and (I) often went upon juries and kept out of the way that I might gradually withdraw for my own ease and their, *John and Robert Laurie's,* benefit.

Several of my friends in the City had often joked me about being sheriff. Thinking this would give a good reason for my withdrawing from business and being suitable to my own ambition, a laudable ambition in every man to rise in society, I consented to stand or take to the office if chosen. My friends Mr D. Richardson and James Thomson got my name introduced upon the Lord Mayor Heygate list. I was drank to as it is called. As the chief magistrates are very often brought in contact with the sheriffs, the sheriffs being only well dressed companions of the Lord Mayor[61], I was anxious to know if the alderman next in rotation, Waithman, had any friends of his own whom he wished to serve with him. I called upon him and he kindly said he would rather I served with him than any one else and that if I had not been nominated by the Lord Mayor he would have proposed me from the hustings Guildhall. Finding that Mr Whittaker was spoken of as the most likely to serve the office, I called upon him and met with the same reception as I had from Mr Waithman. We dined together at Waithman's. All was well arranged and on the 24 June 1823 the Livery elected *with great applause* Peter Laurie and George Whittaker, but as Mr Whittaker's name was first on the nomination list the Court of Aldermen confessed the election only made Whittaker senior sheriff.

This was a proud day to me, I never thought I had so many zealous friends as ever assembled that day in the hall. I immediately appointed Mr D. Richardson my under sheriff as a reward for his zealous exertions. After this numerous invitations followed, I was canvassed as sheriff elect but my health, which never allowed me to feast, compelled me to decline the half of them. I went however to Sir C. Flowers' public breakfast and to one of the delightful trips up the river, the scene ever to me like enchantment, and is one of the greatest treats connected with the Corporation. The two sheriffs now began to order our carriages, liveries etc and on the 28 we were sworn into office, amidst the cheering of our friends although this year it was Sunday. Having been much used to large dinner parties I found less difficulties than most men who take the office and mix in public life for the first *time*.

Having received great marks of kindness from the family of Mr Barrett, Vauxhall, I offered to make Dr Barrett my chaplain which he gladly accepted and was very dignified in his office. On the 29 *September* we presided at Guildhall, Waithman chosen mayor, we than dined Mansion House. On Tuesday the 30th we were presented to the Chief Baron and returned to a splendid dinner Stationers' Hall, had Lord Erskine, Canning, G. Lamb, Huskinsson (sic) etc etc. Thursday went and took possession of the prisons and then went through all the duties which are detailed in Letts diary kept daily by me and not worth repeating in this book. My business from its nature led me daily into conversation with the nobility etc in the most unreserved terms. My office of sheriff leading me to mix with all clases, bishops, judges and I was perfectly at my ease. But the poor unfortunate creature who suffered the extreme sentence of the law was a new class to me. My duty was painful but the wretched men seemed less distressed than I could have imagined.

Before the termination of 1823 I got a free pardon for Barden and Elgar, which gave great satisfaction. There appeared to me no terror in the mind of any convict but the convict doomed to suffer the extreme sentence, in the language of scripture 'all that a man has he will give for his life'. No punishment will deter from great crimes but death. I found the mode of tying the rope to the beam after it had been put round the poor culprit's neck occasioned much unnecessary delay and[62] the executioner often nearly stupid by intoxication. I had the beam made with suspended links and a hook to the rope and the fastening was done in a moment. This simple alteration made great noise in the newspapers and got me much credit.

A society for the protection of trade of which I had been twice president and a very active member met and voted me a very complimentary address which was published in the 'Morning Post' and was gratifying to my feelings after being a member many years. This address was afterwards printed and circulated in my ward when I became a candidate and proves how often small matters may be used to advantage.

Waithman mayor.
At a meeting or assembly of the Lord Mayor, aldermen and Livery of the several Companies of the City of London assembled at their hall, Guildhall, on Wednesday the 29 September 1824.

'Resolved unanimousley that the thanks of this Common Hall be given to George Whittaker Esq. and Sir Peter Laurie Knt., sheriffs of London and sheriffs of Middlesex for very active exertions and unwearied assiuity evinced by them during the year last past, for the humanity and extensive charity displayed towards the unfortunate persons commended to their charge and custody, for their liberality and hospitality in maintaining the honor and dignity of their office, and for the firmness with which they have supported the rights and priviledged of this city.'

1824
I began this year attending daily to the duties of sheriff leaving my business to my two nephews, partners who were very attentive, and left my whole time to be disposed of to the advantage of the City, and the kindess I experienced made me *do* them all the service in my power.

Early this year I saw by the proceedings at the Old Bailey that if a prosecution was not properly described in the indictment it fell to the ground and recollecting that, although John and Robert Peter Laurie were well known by that name, yet as they were my sister's sons their name was Snaddon. And after many enquiries of the many legal men I now daily met, and I never for one moment forgot to benefit all my relations in every possibly way, I went to Mr Capper of the Home Office and he kindly gave me a form[63] which I availed myself of, and presented it to Mr Peel, who very kindly got the sign manual from His Majesty and their names became Laurie legally. And I had the satisfaction of presenting this to them, which was the greatest gift I could bestow as my name was so well known, and as the business was so very productive and this step secured it to them and I hope that with common attention they will reach a good fortune.

At this time I had no immediate prospect of being an alderman and wishing to carry into private life a proof that I had been sheriff my friends suggested to me that I should be knighted, and for this purpose one of them saw a person high in authority in these matters, at least we thought so, Sir George Naylor. He recommended writing to Mr Peel. I was thus reluctantly compelled to see Mr Peel. I say reluctantly for although I was anxious to have the honor I did not like the interview. Mr Peel said it was a very mistaken notion to suppose that because a man was sheriff he thought he could be knighted. There had none been so honor'd since 1807. Upon an address I begged the matter might never be again thought of.

But on the 6 April I had a letter from Mr Peel saying His Majesty intended to honor me with knighthood at the levee the following day. I thought this was a hoax but went immediately to Mr Capper who said it was a genuine letter. I mentioned the subject to no one although I had been at the Old Bailey at breakfast and was in conversation with all who came to the Old Bailey that I knew. I went home at 12, dressed, went to the levee and waited to see Mr Peel, who told me not to write on my card 'to be knighted' as formerly had been the custom, but that he would introduce me to the King. I went round with the company, trembling not knowing how to act. At last Mr Peel introduced me and I dropt upon my knee. The King asked my name, I replied 'Peter'. I thought the King smiled but whether it was at me or my name I could not tell. He then asked the Duke of Montrose for his sword which he waved over my frightened head and said, 'Rise, Sir Peter'. I then drove home, kissed my wife and said she was a Lady at which she, like myself, was *much* affected with His Majesty's condescension and our own good fortune.

We dined with a large party in the City, Mr Brook's, at the City of London Tavern and went to Mrs Heygate's evening party, but there was a large party dining at the Covent Garden *Fund* annual dinner and the Duke of York mentioned it publickly, and someone then came to Heygate's and we were congratulated by our numerous friends. The expences was £108 2s 8d for puting in 'Gazette' and 'Heralds College'. The publication of this very unexpected honor being the first ever conferred wihout any address or public occasion[64] brought to us many letters of congratulation and many old friends laughed heartily when they called me Sir Peter for the first time. The Duke of Sussex said it was the name of a famous horse. This event created a little envy in several quarters in the City, particularly amongst the Liberals who thought I had become a slave; little did they know that no condition was either offered on my part, nor asked by Mr Peel.

There was a drawing room announced and we were most anxious to have the entreé. The Lord Mayor and I saw the Lord Chamberlain, Duke of Montrose, who said it never had been given at St James', advised me to examine the records and if I could point out any instance we should have it. I found there never had been; but at Carlton House and Buckingham House they had assumed, done it and was not questioned. This has since been done at St James's and on the 20 May we attended the drawing room, when Lady Laurie was introduced by the late Lady Mayoress and was saluted by His Majesty, was very pleased and very gratified.

On the 12 June the Lord Mayor and sheriffs dined with the Archbishop of Canterbury and having all the splendid dinners of the year this was the most splendid and costly. A livery servant to each guest. I could not avoid saying to Mr Jenkinson, now a bishop, that had the immense resources which allowed such luxury been divided, like the Scots, amongst the clergy, it would be better for religion. He said no, for there would then be no inducement for *gentlemen* going into the church, it would be in England as in Scotland none but from the lowest ranks would go into the church, etc etc. When the health of the preacher for the society, 'Society for Promoting Christian Knowledge', was given, the mighty chief at the top of the table made a signal, the folding doors flew open and the tea and coffee was seen in the hands of the servants and the preacher could not inflict a speech upon us; we left at 9 having sat down at 7. It was a stiff formal party and the clergymen were afraid to speak, only whispered to each other. They were servile in the extreme.

On the 20 had the judges at my hall, dined at 4 o'clock and a very cheerful afternoon, no toasts or speeches being Sunday. On the 1 June many of the Scotts nobility attended Mr Traing's church, we then went in grand procession to lay the first stone of the new national Scots church, Lord Breadalbane laid the first stone. A gratifying day and an interesting sight to find the nobles joining in erecting a church in England for the benefit of those who prefer the religion of their fathers. Went on 14 August to Margate, Ramsgate, Canterbury, 3 days. The effect of the first day steam packet made me so ill that I was very unwell all the time and glad to get home. Peter was with me. Had the heavy sessions of September. In July the 2 courts of the Old Bailey were opened. The City Lands committee took to themselves the gallery in the new court. This was infringing upon the privilege of the sheriffs. I broke the bar, set upon both the door keepers before the Lord Mayor, who threatened to commit them to Newgate and the City Lands gave up the gallery.

On the 29 September I received a very full and gratifying vote of thanks, on the 1st October at the sheriffs' dinner made my farewell speech and on 5 October went off to France, a journal of which was well kept by Peter, which see, anyone who wishes to see it. On the 20 November returned from France having only been as far as Dijon the weather being so unfavourable. Slept at Dover, had my horses to meet me at Brighton where I remained, hunting and enjoying hunting untill the 22 when I got home to Park Square and we were all very glad to return in health and in good condition. I have forgotten in the proper place to mention that the Mayor and sheriffs this year had the distinguished honor of dining with the Duke of Sussex at Kensington Palace, and I have to remark that at all times I received the greatest kindness from the Duke.

This year purchased 4 houses from Mr Nurse, 3 in Park Square and one in Ulster Terrace, the 3 a good bargain, one of which I intended for my own residence because it had a 4 stall stable and I watched the building of it.

1825

Having now no occupation, I tried several horses, bought one and began hunting in Surrey and received two or three invitations from the Lord Mayor, Garrett, to the Mansion House. Bought houses in the Park and attended my duties as a director of the Beacon Fire Office, which was losing money hourly. This I soon saw and had to contend against the whole of the directors who were more sanguine than I was, and ultimately they came into my views and broke up the company, but not until we had lost £450 each directors and several proprietors lost nearly their all.

This was the year when speculation was at the alarming height. I was invited to join companies of every kind from great breweries to buying houses and selling corn and[65] coals. I attended all the meetings but generally put such questions on the black side that in several instances I knocked them up to the great annoyance of the secretaries and schemers. But one company I had joined, the Equitable Loan Company, Mr Wilks in the spring of 1824 had written to me and stated that I had been nominated as a director. I was at first displeased at this but when I called upon Mr Wilks and saw 27 vice-presidents Members of Parliament, I was pleased with the appointment, and during 1825 we were daily employed in applying to parliament for an act of incorporation, and at the same time trying to obtain a charter. In all this we spent all the deposits, between 30 and 40,000, and this company was afterwards desolved and took many years to arrange all matters respecting it.

This year a friend in the vestry of Marlebone suggested that I would be pleased if I could get a seat in the vestry. I thought so too but knowing it was nearly as difficult to obtain as a seat in the House of Commons I was afraid of becoming a candidate. However Mr Austin, my friend, said he was sure of bringing me in if I would canvass. I did so and had the honor, an honor I am proud of, of being elected with 56 votes, *29 March 1825*, which brought me into company every Saturday with the first people of the country. For the first year or two I was a very silent member, but I soon afterwards became a bit of a leader, for of all gifts, the gift of talking upon your legs seems the most advantageous. And was in April elected, unanimously and at the head of the list, a trustee of the roads. These honors were thrusting themselves upon me. I attended the juries, and that I might not be forgotten in the City I gave a dinner to the Lord Mayor Garrett, Aldermen Brown, Crowder, Scholey, Crowder, Sir C. Flowers, Pollock etc. And in May attended a trial at Bar, 4 knights, Birnie, Alderson, Williams and myself in full dress with swords, a very unusual sight and made a little noise in the papers.

My cousin, Mr John Laurie came from New York and I was much pleased with my relation. He is a genteel man and I took him every where, to Epsom, to the ceremony of laying the first stone of London Bridge, dining on the same day by invitation of Alderman Garrett, the Lord Mayor. A splendid day and for the extraordinary expence the City only voted the Alderman a medal, a very inadequate return.

Went to Cheltenham for the first time in my own carriage and post horses, but found it not half so[66] pleasant as the stage. Took a house and spent our time as all idlers at that idle and attractive place usually do. On the 8th August I had a letter from London stating that Alderman Crowder had resolved to resign his office as alderman and I was solicited to become a candidate. I came to town and as far as I could removed the fears of the worthy Alderman and he promised to serve the office of sheriff, if he declined to do so he was to write to me. I left London and he serviced the office, and we took a tour passing through Tainton, Exeter to Plymouth, Tavistock, returning by Sidmouth, Weymouth and Portsmouth.

Being always anxious to become a magistrate for Middlesex and having received great kindness from Mr Canning, I wrote to that gentleman who forwarded my letter to the Duke of Portland. The Duke[67] wrote 1 October that he had recommended me to the Lord Chancellor for my name to be inserted in the commission of peace for Middlesex and Westminster. And on the 24 October I had the satisfaction of qualifying at Hicks's Hall, paid my fees £5 8s 6d and my £15 15s, the subscription to the dinners, dined and was delighted with the magistrates. They were so kind and polite to me and seemed glad to see me amongst them and nothing, except being elected an alderman[68], gave me more satisfaction than this honorable appointment. I should also except the honor of knighthood. Paid at the Crown Office £3 7s 6d for my Dedimus, and on the 1st November I took my seat at the Court House, Marlebone as a magistrate of the district and on the 5 November took my seat as a Westminster magistrate and paid subscription £16 6s. Thus my magisterial appointment cost me £40 17s and never did I pay money more cheerfully. Dined with the Lord Mayor, Venables, 9 November, many distinguished guests. Hunted with the Berkeley stag hounds. Had a bad fall by Tom not clearing a ditch. Went on 23 to Brighton and enjoyed the superior hunting there, the finest hunting in the world during the remainder of the year.

1826

Returned from Brighton 10 January. Let one of my houses to Mr Slater and amused myself by going to Oxford Street and seeing my friends. The latter part of last year was called the 'year of the panic' and I was very much gratified at assisting one of my friends in the hour of need as he was chiefly the cause of my going into business. How delightful it is to have it in our power to be grateful. In February I rode 60 miles after a stag with Lord Derby. The heaviest rain I can recollect. Got cold myself and nearly ruined my good horse Rattler. Having let my house in Cornwall Terrace[69] for Hugh Munro I was now fully occupied in getting my house, 7, Park Square, ready by the 25 March and having completed it by that day we took possession and was much pleased with the change of residence, particularly with the stable. This spring I was put in the new Commission of Sewers for Westminster, a very important commission, and took my seat at the board accordingly. I was thus upon every important commission in Middlesex and Westminster. We, the directors of the Caledonian asylum, selected ground for the new asylum.

At the anniversary of the 'Highland School Society' I took the chair and the way I gave Mr Hume's health as one of the most industrious and honest M.P.s gave the 'Courier' great offence which made them show me up, and I called, saw the editor, who said he had no dislike to me but took that opportunity and every opportunity he could of exposing and showing up. Joseph said any letter I might write he would insert. I did so and stated my public principles, dated 2nd June 1826, wherein I stated I was friendly to reform but a great enemy of the emancipation of the Roman Catholics.

Mr Alderman Cox's death

Times was now approaching, what was very interesting to me. On the 21 June the gig was at the door, I was going on a jury, but saw in the 'Times' the sudden death of Alderman Cox, and as my eye was fixed on Aldersgate thinking Mr Cox would resign, and knowing some of the Common Council, I turned my horse's head to the City instead of Westminster Hall. Went with Mr Richardson my late under sheriff, saw Rolles, Matthews, Diggins, and they resolved to call a meeting of the inhabitants on the following day. The inhabitants accordingly met and resolved to adjourn the meeting until the next day, to see if a candidate could be found in the ward. I gave the 'Courier' to know my public opinions. On the 23, Friday, they again met, and adjourned till Monday, Mr Peto, to whom I was strongly recommended by[70] Mr Henry Richardson, afterwards sheriff. I was not admitted, but I was taken up by a committee or little band, as I termed them and they went round the ward with me. I had many promises, and was often overwhelmed by the unexpected and overpowering kindness of the generous inhabitants. We went and had a lunch at the Albion before we started, and dined at the close of the canvass at the Castle and Falcon, where Mr Smith, Mr Nicols, Mr Deputy Fisher's son, and many zealous friends joined and we considered my success certain. Four candidates started: Sir J. Williams, Pearson, Mr Morrison and Farebrother. On the Saturday took lunch at the Castle and Falcon, canvassed those which were not seen the day before. The day was the hottest I ever felt. The committee issued the following:

Aldersgate ward
At a very numerous and highly respectable meeting of freemen of this ward, friends of Sir Peter Laurie. Held at the Albion House, Aldersgate Street Friday *23 June 1826*. Mr John Rolls in the chair. It was moved by Mr Sewell and seconded by Mr Wickes and resolved unanimously:

'That Sir Peter Laurie is in the opinion of this meeting in every respect eligible to be elected alderman of this ward, his ample fortune, his strict integrity, his general urbanity of manners, his constitutional principles and activity of mind being strong recommendations for our support and confidence, we do recommend him to our brother freemen of the ward as a fit and proper person to represent us in the Court of Aldermen.

'That a committee be now formed for the purpose of commencing an immediate and active canvass.'
John Rolls, chairman.Committee room, Albion House. 23 June 1826.

'To the worthy and independent inhabitants of the ward of Aldersgate[71].
Gentlemen,
The lamented death of Mr Alderman Cox having occasioned a vacancy in your respectable ward, I beg leave to offer myself as a candidate to fill that important office. I am not, you are aware, an untried citizen presenting myself to your notice for the first time. As one of your late sheriffs and as a magistrate for the county you are well enabled to judge how fit I may be for the prompt and willing discharge of the responsible duties of that honorable station for which I now solict your sufferages. My time, being wholly unfettered by business of any kind, shall be devoted with whatever talents I possess to promote the interest and protect the rights and privileges of my constituents and fellow citizens. Should I have the honor of being elected I pledge myself to the active and punctual discharge of all the duties which will thus devolve upon me and being entirely regardless of all personal considerations, I will not retain the gown an hour longer than I am able to do justice to the numerous and constant claims which the electors of every ward have upon the time and attention of their alderman.

I have the honour to be, gentlemen, your obedient and humble
Peter Laurie.
7, Park Square. 21 June 1826.

Card: Vote for Sir Peter Laurie, the friend of the public charities, humanity, the privileges of the citizens, the dignity of the Corporation, the tried protector of trade and commerce.

Such were the hasty papers circulated. The precept came from the Lord Mayor Venables, for the election to take place at 9 o'clock on Monday the 27 June 1826 and the ward clerk sent a circular calling the inhabitants of the ward together at 12 o'clock Monday to consider of a fit and proper person to fill the office of alderman. I attended at the Albion when my friends who had signed a requisition came and stated the meeting wished to see me. I accordingly entered the room and was received with three cheers. The reception I met with quite overcame my feelings. My nomination was moved by Mr Peto and seconded by Mr Rolls. It was received with loud shouts of acclamation and after I could speak I returned my thanks in a grateful manner. Mr Morrison was also proposed and seconded but was withdrawn, as he said he would not disturbe the unanimity of the ward, and said they could not have made a better choice.

On the following day, the 27 June, I arrived at the dispensary room where the elections are all held at ¼ before 9 o'clock and the Lord Mayor came in state at 9. Mr Peto proposed and Mr Rolls seconded. Noone else was proposed and my election was by acclamation. I left the room with the Lord Mayor. It is worthy of remark that the Lord Mayor did not congratulate the ward nor myself and it was evident to me and all present that he was mortified at the unanimous election. Messers Wood and Waithman wrote to the King to get Morrison elected as a man they could depend upon to vote with them on all public questions. Yet I think Waithman was not upon the whole disappointed at my election. The weather very hot.

On the 30 the Common Cryer called and I paid him his fee 46/4d. And on the 4 July, 155 of the principal inhabitants of the ward gave me a grand dinner, I had my school fellow Colonel Forrest. And on the 6th, there was a Court of Aldermen, I was presented by the deputies for I had confirmed the appointment made by Alderman Cox of Mr Fisher and Mr Lorkin and the other Common Councilmen and Mr King and[72] other gentlemen of the ward. I went home with the Lord Mayor in the state coach and we had a dinner at the Mansion House. And on the 18 July I gave my dinner to 118 of the inhabitants, had Sinclair to sing, all went off well, and the whole cost including £72 to school and hospitality about £300, as entered in expenses book, exclusion of cloaks for self or beadles. And on Wednesday the 19, went with the Lord Mayor's party up the river and was now fully installed as a magistrate of London. And the most gratifying circumstance was that I was elected unanimously and on the first vacancy after I had been sheriff.

I declined joining the Lord Mayor's party to Oxford, but joined them at Windsor, slept there and came to London in the barge. All very pleasant and had the good fortune not to be mentioned in the chaplain's celebrated tour to Oxford. And after my great anxiety and fatigue we set of for Ramsgate. *4 August*, took a house at Broadstairs where we remained some time enjoying rides alternately to Ramsgate and Margate and on the 21 slept at Dover. Came round the coast by Hastings, Tunbridge etc. Reached London 28 August. And on the

5 September Lady Laurie went to Worthing to see her sisters. I joined them on the 16 at Worthing.

Deputy Lieutenant, Middlesex

The Duke of Portland had kindly not only recommended me as a magistrate, but appointed me a deputy Lieutenant of Middlesex, and on the 3 October I attended at Guildhall, Westminster as one of the deputy Lieutenants *of Middlesex*. This honorable appointment enables me to wear the cockade in my servant's hats, but to wear the button, and since the militia have not been called out, ours is only an honorary one[73]. Nothing occurred in September or October. The usual swearing in of new sheriffs, new Mayor, Brown, etc and in November I went several times into Surrey and hunted with Jolliff, the harriers etc etc. At Christ's Hospital I nominated Mr Daniel Richardson to be a governor for £200 instead of £400. This is the privilege of the alderman, and I did this for Mr Richardson in consequence of his zealous exertions to get me elected an alderman. On the 21 December, St Thomas's day, I held my first wardmote when all the old Common Council were elected, except Lloyd resigned. Rolls and Mottram went to a poll and at the close (of) the 3d day Rolls was 12 ahead of Mottram. Had them all to dine with me on that day, a custom which I intend to keep up as long as I am an alderman.

1827

This year I began my very extensive duties as an alderman where I was constant in my attendance[74] and also as a magistrate of Middlesex and Westminster. The last I gradually discontinued, but having met with such great kindness from my brothers in the commission I fully determined never to give up attending the county courts. A question now began to agitate the county, by building a lunatic asylum, brought on by Lord Robert Seymour who took me to Bedlam, Warburton's private mad house, where I saw such misery that I resolved never if possible to witness such scenes again, but resolved to support Lord Robert. In the county courts, 1 committee was formed I was included. A motion was made by Mr Chambers to have the court opened to the public, seconded by myself, we had but 15 votes. But Mr Haines called at the close of the debate, I walked with him round Smithfield and gave from memory all the speeches and they appeared most accurately in the paper next day. I afterwards dined with the magistrates, went home 10 o'clock and (none) suspected me. This I repeated at another meeting of the magistrates. It was then said we may as well open the court as the reports got abroad and I think I was suspected the 2nd time but no one asked me. At the next county court Colonel Wood moved that it be opened, I seconded it: it was carried. Thus did such an honorable man as myself throw open that court and the result has been most beneficial to the public. Of the committee of 15 the question for the asylum was carried and I had the honor of being appointed one.

Early this year the Duke of York died and as I loved that prince I went in procession at his funeral, 20 January. Having often been upon lunacy juries and thinking we were always too willing to give implicit credit to the medical men and as there was one when the property was great and the investigation continued 7 days, I had determined to bring in a verdict of lucid intervals. And during the whole period of the investigation I examined the witnesses to that effect and had the good fortune to get most of (the) jury to agree with me, although we had Scarlet against us and Denman for us. Part of the jury stood out for a day but at last we brought in the verdict of insanity with lucid intervals. This was opposed by the commissioners, and in fact the verdict was of no use to the brother, who wished to set aside a marriage with an improper person. The result was I got the verdict, but was never summoned again upon any lunacy jury.

In consequence of my being elected alderman my Company, the Saddlers', elected me on the Court as is usual when their liverymen are made magistrates. And on the 1 March I was sworn in, and dined with the Company, a Company that has but one fault; they have too many dinners, about 40, in the year. On the 2d the ministers dined with the Lord Mayor in court mourning, the first dinner since I became a magistrate. Mr George Laurie my cousin came from America and I was much pleased with him. I had not seen him for 20 years. I introduced him everywhere and regretted that two such friends should live at so great a distance. I wish they lived in London as they, he and his brother, are a credit to the name of Laurie.

Attended several river parties which are delightful. And on the 10 July left London for Dover[75]. Lady Laurie, Peter and I, we went to Calais, Bruges, Ghend, Antwerp, Brussels Spa, Aix La Chapel, Colonge, Coblenz, Bergen, Frankfurt, Dramstad, Bruchell, Offenburgh, thro the Black Forest, Hofhausen, Zurich, Bern, Morat, Lausanne, Geneva, La Battay, Poliquy, Dole, Dijon, Avallon, Auxerre, Lens, Fountainbleau, Paris, Beauvois, Abbeville, Boulonge, Calais, London. The particulars of this journey is well described in Peter's journal, regularly kept by him.

Attended the September sessions, being on the rota on the 1st October. Upon my return from the presentation of the sheriffs at Westminster, it was very wet and boards laid upon the bed of the river at the side and while running upon the boards one of them tilted and I broke the tendon of my leg. The feeling was as if a sharp stone had been thrown at my leg, but I could not walk. I went to Stationers' Hall and sent for Mr Woodthorpe's crutches, called and brought Pettigrew home with me. Had a splint part of my leg, was confined to my room from the 1st to the 19th, when I went to Mr Hills to tea. And on the 27 I went to Cambridge to introduce Peter to his college, but was very lame and nothing but my regard for him could have induced me to leave home. My leg was not painful, only very troublesome and I read much during the time; Scot's 'Life of Bounapart' which I never should have read but for my long confinement.

This year Mrs Jack died, *wife of William*, and I got an arrangement with Mr De Bott, the residuary legatee and had all arranged to the satisfaction of all parties and the Misses Jacks and Lady Laurie had their share of their late uncle's property. And at the close of the year my friend Dr Waugh died and I went to the grave with him. I do not recollect the loss of a good man so severly felt as the loss of Dr Waugh. I had long been intimate with him. He blended piety, good humour and good will to all mankind in an extraordinary degree, not equalled by any man I ever saw[76]. Nothing further took place during 1827 of any importance. Not being able to mount or dismount easily I this year did not go to Brighton, therefore lost the hunting this year at that delightful place.

1828

This year my mind became much harrassed by an application to pay the Commercial Bank of Scotland, to pay £5,000. The Rev. Mr Thomson, Coldstream, wished his brother-in-law to be agent for the bank at Coldstream and as the bank wished a better security or at least one better known, I signed the cautionary bond and had a counter-security from the Reverend Mr Alex Thomson. This was in (blank) and in the close of 1827 the agent stopped payment. This application I resisted upon the grounds that I was answerable for all bills discovered but not bills renewed, and when Thomson became agent the drawers were full of dishonored bills and they got or suffered Thomson to renew all those bills, and then came upon the cautioners. This I determined to resist, I employed Mr Pirie, attorney, Mr Davis. The bank commenced an action in the King's Bench. I retained Mr Brougham and Mr D. Pollock made the jury speech. I communicated with Messers Dallas and Innes, Edinburgh, who advised arbitration. This I would have agreed to had I been in Scotland, but thinking myself sure of success in[77] the King's Bench, I still persisted in my firm determination and hope I am right, although the subject has given me much uneasiness.

In March Mr Whittaker and I called upon Mr Newman, *City*, and got our small balance. Thus it required 4 years to wind up our sheriffs' accounts. The penal settlement for the county, July same year. I have no recollection of anything particular this year. I did my routine of duty as a magistrate etc etc.

We went on the 7 August to Cheltenham, had a house, Cambray, at 5 and a half guineas per week, had 2 *saddle* horses and coachman with us, on the 26 went to Malvern then to Leamington. Returned by Stowe and got to London on the 5 September to attend the Old Bailey sessions.

And on the 12 November we set of for Brighton, took a house, 3 Lower Rock Gardens, 6 guineas per week, had 3 horses, hunted until the 18 December when we reached home. On the 20 I received £300 from the *treasurer* J.C. Herries on account of the Equitable Loan Company, which enabled to pay some of the numerous creditors, and I believe Mr Herries when he wrote that it was my name which inclined him to pay the same.

1829

Mr Leslie having charged the trustees of Swallow Street with not giving an account of all monies received at the doors etc, and the trustees being the late Messers Nelson, Neven and Jack, I got from Mr Birnie a bond to save Lady Laurie and the Miss Jacks. Harmless, I allowed the enquiry to go on and Mr Leslie was defeated in the Court of Chancery. I believe the trustees gave much money from their own pockets and received none. On the 19th January the Duke of Wellington and the other ministers dined Mansion House. Nothing occurred but the usual routine of duty, dining etc, as entered in Letts's diary. Robert (Peter), having in my opinion formed a low connexion, I would not see him until he agreed to break it off and did not see him for some time. Went on the *24 July* to Rochester. Met the Lord Mayor, dined, viewed the boundry and returned by land, 25, a splendid part. Peter and I went off to Birmingham 13 August. Slept at the Nelson, then took a tour through Shrewsbury, Chester, Bangor, viewed Menai Bridge, afterwards went to Carnarvon, Aberystwith, Carmarthen, Swansea, Gloster, remained 3 days at Cheltenham.

On the 28 went to Gravesend, dined and next day viewed the Thames and Medway canal. After a sumtuous breakfast with the Mayor and magistrates of Gravesend, dined at 3 on the 29, and came home with Newman and Tyrell.

This day, 31 August 1829, I signed an agreement with John Laurie relinquishing in his favor my share of the trade in Oxford Street stock in trade, book debts etc, giving a lease of my whole time of Oxford Street for the consideration of £6,725 and received a bond for the amount. But as a condition I caused to be inserted in the partnership deeds of John and Robert Laurie, that Robert was, at the end of 7 years, to have the half and to pay for the additional share what by arbitration should be considered a fair price, thus as far as I could protecting Robert's interest, but I was thus making a great sacrifice giving up one of the best and most productive concerns I knew.

On the 26 September Mr Alderman Crowder wrote to me that he could not and would not take upon himself of the office of mayor. This came upon me like a thunder bolt and after all the City authorities being consulted, it was resolved to press Mr Crowder to stand and after seeing him daily at last he agreed to stand and Crowder was elected on the 29, but to me they were very uneasy and uncomfortable days, having made no preparations and Key having got excused for one year.

On the 19th November we set of for Brighton and took up our abode at 76 King's Road at 5½ guineas per week, and had 3 horses. Bad weather. Hunted often notwithstanding the weather and returned 17 December.

I should have mentioned in the proper place that on the 28 February I made a speech against the Roman Catholic claims which induced the 'Morning Post' to send to me for a copy which I furnished and was published and Mr O'Connel began a series of letters addressed to me in the 'Herald', but only one was published. I refused to dine in the Mansion House when the Lord Mayor gave a dinner to Peel upon his receiving the freedom of the City, such was my protestant zeal.

1830

This year Alderman Crowder being unwell I sat at the Mansion House for 6 weeks. During the whole of that period it was a hard frost and I walked nearly every day into the City. In the spring of this year[78] I proposed my nephew for the livery of my Company but to my astonishment the court said as he was not a trade nor could I say, although he had been bound to me, that he had served a regular apprenticeship, he could not as a matter of right be admitted. Yet they very kindly admitted him as a matter of favor.

This year was established a new club, the 'Literary Union'. I was invited to become a member, but as I always had objected to a ballot I refused unless I was admitted as an original member. I was so admitted, and found it very pleasant, giving me the opportunity of meeting genteel, well-informed men. The struggle to get in became very great, and the club became prosperous.

Having several years before this period become very intimate with Mr Wilkie, his sister and brother, the intimacy became very great between Lady Laurie and Miss Wilkie. This was to me very satisfactory, as in Miss Wilkie we found an excellent, well-informed, kind and affectionate friend and unless we saw her every two or three days it was a great blank in our society, and I found in Mr Wilkie all that I could wish in an intelligent friend.

James Laurie who had been brought up as a coachmaker, I got to a respectable coachmakers, coming to dine with us on Sunday. I, after I thought he was sufficiently improved in his business, got him a free merchant's indenture at the India House from Mr Ker, Mr Alexander's partner, and after fitting him out he sailed for India, which cost altogether nearly £200. Peter Laurie have now attained his majority, altho the coming of age was of no service to him as he had no patrimony to receive. I got him, with great difficulty, upon the Livery of the Saddlers' Company. He was objected to not having been brought up to the trade. I however stood so well with the court[79] he was admitted.

April 15, while riding with Lady Laurie on horseback the grey mare she rode reared and falling back upon Lady Laurie broke her collarbone and five ribs. Mr Wright who saw the dreadful accident came home with Lady Laurie, sent for Pettigrew who came and bandaged the body and shoulders. Mrs Pettigrew remained all night. Miss Wilkie came and remained with Lady Laurie nearly the whole time she was dangerously ill and was unrepented of her kindness. Many enquiries after Lady Laurie.

This year Dr Spry recommended me to the vestry to be churchwarden, the highest office they could confer and I had the honor to be unanimously elected and continued to discharge the duties and sat in the parish church during the whole of my year of office, but to me it was a painful one as I was called upon to preside at public meetings, the first to pass resolutions expressive of the joy the radicals wished to exhibit to the country at the French revolution. This I first agreed to do but finding there was no precedent for the churchwarden taking the chair, I declined. I was again and again solicited to, to take the chair upon political subjects, all of which I declined, and this raised up a host of political enemies, not only in the parish, but all over London, and which made me deeply regret that I ever became churchwarden of St Marylebone parish. Upon the death of George the 4th, all my good fortune left me.

Candidate for the City

It being generally understood that my principal reason for becoming an alderman was ultimately to represent the City, when William the 4th ascended the throne the consequence was a new parliament, many friends applied to me. But upon considering all matters I thought it would be a hard struggle and as all the members stood again it would be like opposing myself to them all. I, after mature reflection, inserted the following address.

7, Park Square. 6 July 1830.

To the *worthy and independent* Livery of London.

Gentlemen, I have received so many and repeated solicitations from highly respectable and influential individuals to declare myself a candidate for your sufferages at the ensuing general election that were I activated by mere personal views of ambition, I should not for a moment hesitate in soliciting your general support, but it is due to their kind partiality at once to state that unless some other gentleman comes forward to oppose the sitting members it is not my intention to disturb the unanimity of the City on the present occasion. Should there, however, be a contest I shall be found at my post. I beg to assure you that whether at this or some future opportunity I should become the object of your choice I shall faithfully and diligently devote my whole time and attention to the various and important duties which devolve on your representative and my most earnest endeavours should be directed to protect and maintain, as far as lies in my power, our ancient privileges, whether private right or corporate franchise, to support the dignity and prerogative of the Crown and to promote the commercial interests of this great city.

I have the honor etc, P. Laurie.

On the day of election I spoke at considerable length from the hustings. Again I was urged to stand, which refused, and pledged myself to stand next time. The proceedings were faithfully reported in the papers of the day; see 'Times' 30 July. King George 4th died 26 June 1830 at ¼ past 3 morning[80]. Rode from vestry, and found the Lord Mayor and aldermen had set off to St James' in their gowns. I followed. All went into the *Privy Council* Chamber. The proclamation was brought into the waiting room when all signed it. We then all returned to the Mansion House and voted an address of condolence. On the

Monday went in state ½ past 10 o'clock and the procession set out to Temple Bar and came to the City, held another Court of Aldermen and voted an address of condolence and congratulation.

July 15. The King's funeral.
17. 22 Aldermen, 160 Common Councilmen reached the palace at 2. At 3 saw the King on the throne surrounded by his court. Asked me how the Scots hospital was coming on. Kissed hands.
22. The grand river party, Dougles's and Lord Mayor's party.
24. City Lands up the river.
August 5. The King went to the Tower. The procession left the Mansion House at 9, met the King at 10 o'clock, Temple Bar, we preceded the King at walking pace, got to the Tower at 12. Had a breakfast with all the members of His Majesty's court, the Queen received introductions. A busy brilient day. I afterwards dined at Blackheath.
11. Set of with post horses at 3 o'clock and took Miss Wilkie with us. Slept at Seven Oaks then Tunbridge Wells and took a tour to Hastings, Brighton and came to Worthing, 18th, and took a house, 5 guineas a week and remained at Worthing till 24 September. During the time I had been at Worthing Key's friends, Mr Legg my informant, were afraid from certain reports that Key was to be rejected and I was to be chosen, and they had anonymous sent to Key, requesting him to be returned with one of the aldermen past the chair and off all things not to allow Laurie to be returned with him. The consequence was he crammed the hall[81], Key and Copeland was returned not with the knowledge of Copeland. I demanded a poll, but it having been represented to me that it was a mistake I abandoned my intention, and dined at the Mansion House. The anonymous letters Key afterward gave me and I have them still[82].
October 27. Crowder gave a grand dinner to the deputation of the Scots church at Mansion House[83]. Dr Chalmers and all were very pleased they came from Scotland with an address from the general assembly of Scotland.

Attended almost daily the committee to prepare Guildhall for the reception of the King and Queen. Dined twice and all went on well until Sunday the 7 November, when the King began to give up the thoughts of coming into the City. The Duke of Wellington sent for Routh, Oldham, Jones and then Key's letter was produced. On Monday attended Court of Aldermen from 11 till 4 considering the letter from Key to the Duke and the King's or rather Peel's letter postponing the King's visit. All the dinner was dressed, all the guests invited and seats arranged. Such a disappointment never was before known and the print shops exposed the folly of the assembly. Key was not sworn in till near 12 o'clock when we all assembled at Guildhall and was there all the 9th, dined there and remained till 11 at night, walking the streets, all quiet.

Nothing occurred during the period from the 9th of November till the 31 December except the change of Ministers, various meetings for reform, but as I thought the measure of reform was rather too extensive I declined attending, hence all the ill will from the ultra's radicals.

Attended 16 December 1830 and proved to the county *of Middlesex* that I had saved the county (£)2000 a year. Crowder died and Kelly elected alderman in his stead.

1831

This has been to me the most painful year I ever recollect and shall detail the usages I have met with.

January. During January I was employed daily for the purpose of getting my excellent friend Mr Wilkie to paint the picture of the King for the Scots hospital. Another painter had been named, but with good luck I succeeded. On the 20 a most uncalled for attack was made upon me by 'Don Key' in the 'Times'. On the 21 I retaliated in strong terms, which he can never get over. As there had been no dinner on the 9th November the Lord Mayor and sheriffs agreed to give two at the Mansion House on the 26. I went and dined at the first dinner, as the sheriffs paid part of the dinner I could not refuse but desired that I should not be introduced. During dinner Key sent to take wine with me. I told the servant that it was a mistake; this gave great offence. On the 28 I went with the City Solicitor and Key and I shaked hands, he having declared that the words reported were the reporter's and not his. On the 29 the Ministers dined at the Mansion House. Shaw elected Chamberlain.

February 9. Got Mr Pirie to agree to serve the office of sheriff and took Cowan and introduced him to Mr Pirie. Then bought a grey horse from Dye for £80.

March 7. Common Hall for election of M.P. for the City, Thompson ratted, Ward was firm to his principles, said he would not support the Reform Bill[84].

The Corporation went with an address to the King for dissolving parliament. sheriffs knighted; Marshall and Poland. Held a wardmote Aldersgate and resolutions passed respecting reform.

24. Went to drawing room, Lady Laurie introduced by Lady Erroll, I was introduced by Duke of Sussex. Lady Laurie the best dressed in the room.

April 25. Laid in 80 dozen port at 54/- and 40 dozen at 44/- which Mr Allnutt sent to the Mansion House. Parliament having been disolved on the 22, the election for the City took place 29 when Waithman, Wood, Thompson and Venables were elected.

May. The King having agreed to dine in the City, great preparations were made. On the 4 May it was stated the King would not come and on the 5 a lame excuse was made for postponment of the King's visit. On the 12th, a Common Council was held and resolution passed hoping the King would still come into the City, but were much disappointed at the refusal.

June 21. I moved in the Court of Aldermen that the Jews be admitted to the freedom, and carried my motion.

24. Cowan and Pirie chosen by show of hands for sheriffs. Scales demanded a

poll. This was to me very gratifying as Pirie served solely to oblige me. The poll was abandoned by Scales who soon saw that he had no chance. On the evening went to Lady Bucley's fancy ball, a most splendid sight, persons of the greatest respectability dressed in all the costumes of the world.

30. Peter Laurie this day qualified as a Middlesex magistrate, the Duke of Portland having kindly put him in the commission of the peace and I believe the youngest man he ever put into the peace.

July 6. This day I dined with the East India directors who gave a splendid dinner to Rahmoun Roy who made a very brilliant speech in favor of the East India Company and fearing he might make a very different statement elsewhere, I sent for Haynes the reporter and gave him an account of the dinner and an excellent account was given, including Roy's speech.

August 1. This was the long looked for day when the King and Queen were to open London Bridge. It was a fine morning, the whole of London in a bustle. Lady Laurie, Miss Wilkie and myself in my chariot, Mr Wilkie and Peter in a glass coach. Started ¼ after 1 o'clock to the Southwark side. The arrangement of the tents, tables etc, were the grandest and beautiful that could be seen. King etc came ½ past 3. Walked over the bridge and saw Mr Crawshaw go up in a balloon. King and party went away ½ past 6. Every eye was gratified, every mind delighted, and I think it was the most splendid and enchanting sight ever witnessed.

4. Dined at the Skinner'(s Company). Key said to me that the 8 of November would be the happiest day he ever saw so tired was he of his office. Yet at the same time, *he* had long before that period, he had been seeking any to get a second year.

5. Peter and I went by the 'Retaliator' to the Plough Inn, Cheltenham and remained till the 11, when we went to Bristol, slept at the Bath Hotel Clifton. Returned on the 15, having come thro Bath, Sunday at Reading and got home on the Monday.

20. Miss Wilkie, Lady Laurie, Peter and I went off to Dorking where we remained all the Sunday at a comfortable inn. Reached Brighton 22, Albion, and on the 24 took No.40, Bedford Square at 6 guineas a week. Had 3 horses and rode about Brighton till September 6 when I came to London to Saddlers' Hall. On Thursday the 8 Mr Wesley came in a glass coach at 7, took William, got to Westminster Abbey ¼ before 8. The Abbey nearly full, got the best seats being first and witnessed the coronation, the account of which see newspapers. A wet afternoon. Returned to Brighton Friday the 9th.

Election

September 15. Came up from Brighton to attend the Saddlers' steward's feast. After dinner Mr Woodthorpe, who came with an evening ticket said he was informed that Key was to be proposed for a 2d year. This I laughed at, and returned to Brighton on Friday the 16. On my return to Brighton I found a letter from Mathews saying that Mr Tegg had called upon him and told him of the plot to keep me out. I wrote to Mathews that I would see him on the Monday morning, that I would come up on Sunday.

19. Breakfasted Old Bailey. Attended Common Hall for some political purpose. Had a meeting of friends at Saddlers' Hall, Tegg in the chair. Published the resolution on the 20 and called a meeting for Thursday at the London Tavern which was numerously attended. Mr Herring in the chair. Mr Slade, Weston, Alderman Brown, Easthope, Hart and Copeland addressed the company, passed several resolutions of the same nature as at the Saddlers' Hall. A committee was spontanously formed. Mr James Brougham wrote a note to me at the meeting saying if I spoke out the Chancellor would make Key give it up. Messers Herring and Tegg chairmen, Hart treasurer, Shanklin and Anderton secretaries, and a great zeal everywhere. Messers Easthope and Alderman Wood said they would do what they could with the government to stop the election.

At Pettigrew's where Easthope and James Brougham followed me, a letter was written which I signed. Brougham said he would get the Chancellor to stop Key, for that the most difficult task he had had was to get the King to make Key a baronet and he could not refuse him. However, he was mistaken for neither he nor Pearsons who was sent for by Wylde would give it up, saying they were certain that it had gone too far. Had a meeting at Aldersgate[85] respecting reform and there denied that, that I had said that I would unfurl the banner of anti-reform as had been falsely said by Bodkin and Clarkson and printed in a thousand shapes by the radicals. Dined at the King's Head on the 24 Saturday, where we established a constant sitting of committee, having got polling books, clerks, canvassing books etc. The money flew like dust.

26. In getting out of my gig to call upon Mr Charles Forbes my foot caught the rein and I bruised my knee in a shocking manner. Drove to the committee room, sent for a surgeon, was carried into a coach. This I have no doubt lost me my election, and it was 2 months before I got the use of my leg. I, for one month, lay upon the sofa and had a bed in the library. On the 29th *Thursday* was carried into Guildhall. The hall very full. The show of hands was doubtful, but by a second show the livery returned Key and Thorp. A poll was demanded by my friends. On the Saturday I intended to withdraw but I got to the head of the poll: Key 1653, Laurie 1658, Thorp 1518. My committee called upon me on the Sunday and advised me to go on, and on Thursday the 6 October the final close of the poll was Key 3258, Thorp 3081, Laurie 2713. I resolved not to have a second election. While this was going on the most intense interest was created by the House of Lords discussing the Reform Bill and it was thrown out by a majority of 41 on Saturday the 8th.

October 10. Monday the Court of Aldermen returned Thorp. The streets were full of placards calling me an anti-reformer and Key was exposed respecting Christ's Hospital. I repeatedly wrote and denyed the expressions they accused me of using, such as the dregs of society etc.

14. Friday a second Common Hall[86]. Key's party put up Key and Thompson. Thompson behaved most shamefully. A poll was demanded thinking that we could use a legal disqualification of Thompson if he had refused, and if he said he would serve, the court would elect him, but he would neither say yes nor no. Had no committee, no clerks. On the 7th day the poll was Thompson 2564, Key 2463, Laurie 456, Waithman 36.
24. Court of Aldermen; 12 voted for Thompson, 5 for Key.
25. Wrote an address at Hart's retiring from the contest. On the same day a meeting of Farebrother's was held at the London Tavern resolved to carry all before them. Routh in the chair.
26. Wednesday a Common Hall[87]. I did not attend show. Key and Kelly, Farebrother demanded a poll. On the 3d day the poll was Key 1965, Kelly 1921, Farebrother 644. Farebrother declined on 3d day.
November 4. Friday, Court of Aldermen. Brown, Heygate and Garrett gave in, others did not vote, 11 voted for Key, 4 for Farebrother. Key returned.

Thus terminated one of the most painful 7 weeks I ever experienced, great pain of body and anguish of mind. I had, however, one satisfaction. I polled 2713 of the most respectable livery of London and that during the time of unequalled political excitment. I am writing this just 12 months after the period and the past year has been a most unpleasant one to me. Often, very often did I resolve to resign my office of an alderman and rued the day I ever went into the City, the expence too *of the election* £973 18s 6d was a large sum thrown away. I resolved not to go into the Mansion House until I went there in my own right.
9. The Lord Mayor's day kept but I did not go near it and few aldermen attended, only 5 out of 26, and the meeting was such as one as must have been expected considering the party which obtained the ascendency. At this time the people of all ranks became alarmed about the colera (sic). A meeting at the Mansion House; I would not go under the roof.
15. A Court of Aldermen. No vote of thanks to the Mayor for his conduct as is usual for the past year. Waithman published a pamphlet which Anderton put his name to, called a 'Key to open the wards of the City and an account of Christ's Hospital'.
December 2. This day I voted and by a majority of 3 we carried in Common Council to have a new street from London Bridge to the Mansion House, a very great improvement. Thus terminated a year which was to me from the election and other circumstances connected with the City was the most harassing and unpleasant I ever experienced.

1832

January 3. A Court of Aldermen. Hughes sworn in and dined Mansion House, but such was the honor and consistency of the aldermen only 4, Heygate because it was his duty, Thorp, Wilson and Thompson. This year I have been obliged to go to many dinners and give many dinners and prepare for the election on the next 29 September as my friends with a very few exceptions advised me against resigning my office of alderman.

Was this year very attentive to my duties as a Middlesex magistrate, gave several notices to consider the use and abuse of grand juries and Peter Laurie wrote a pamphlet on the subject which was much praised and was very clever.

North British Life Insurance Company having been very successful in Edinburgh, they resolved to establish a branch in London. We selected 15 names that we thought influential and a grand dinner at the Albion was given on the 18 April. Mr Cockburn in the chair. And on the 9th May we began business when I was unanimously elected chairman of the London board for two years, which is the time by Act of Settlement.

April 23. I had the narrowest escape I ever had for my life. Being Easter Monday the Staines bridge was opened, we had a splendid dinner given by Jolliff and Banks. Peter and I remained till it was dark and had no lamps to the gig, we allowed Rattler a very fast horse to go at his own pace. And at Hounslow a quantity of broken stones[88] had been laid in the centre of the road. The horse, to clear them, went against a post, broke off the iron step. The shock was so great I was thrown to the middle of the road and fell upon my back. Peter was thrown over the head of the horse. We were both considerably bruised, but Peter fortunately kept hold of the rein. The horse did not get away. The gig and harness was knocked to pieces. I took a post chaise at Hounslow, got home and laid up for a few days, not mentioning the accident, but if either of us had been thrown upon our heads, as the pace we were going and the violence of the shock, it must have been instant death.

John Laurie having married a beautiful women, *Miss Mary Sparks*, was delivered of a girl, 17 April. She, the mother, died 23 and *was buried* 28th, a great loss to poor John.

The ministry, having been outvoted in the Lords, resign, the unions and Common Council went and petition the King to keep his Ministers and much agitation prevails in London in May. I abstained from interfering in the proceedings of Common Council. The Duke of Wellington resigns and the ministers take office again, the Lords having agreed that the Reform Bill shall pass, rather that a sufficient number of peers be absented to carry the measure. The Lords absent themselves and the Bill passes.

A Bill having passed to allow the inhabitants of the London parishes to elect their own vestrymen and by that Bill the 3 of Marlebone vestry were lotted out. I was lotted out by the 38 drawn and 40 were lotted out. I thus left the vestry where I had been 7 years and it was the *most* pleasant assembly I was ever in, but perhaps I liked it the better because I had considerable influence in it and I have every reason to think I was greatly respected by the gentlemen present, from the Duke of Portland to the respectable tradesmen, for none but respectable tradesmen were chosen into the old vestry. I was proud of being elected but was not sorry at being lotted out as the new members were so different in all respects from those who were vestrymen upon the old system.

The North British Fire and Life Insurance Office having been established in 1809 in Edinburgh and so successful that it resolved to establish a branch in London, and on the 9th May we the new directors and several of the Edinburgh directors dined at the Albion, the dinner given by the Parlat board. I was unanimously elected chairman of the London board. I joined this company from my good opinion of the talents, integrity of the resident directors, B. and M. Boyd.

The Common Council having voted the freedom of the City to Thomas Attwood esq., a dinner was given by 'Don Key', the mayor, which I did not attend as I liked none of the company.

May 28. King's birthday. Lady Laurie and I went to drawing room. After great exertions to get the Equitable Loan Company affairs closed we had £314 7s 2d in Attwood's bank, but fearing it might be attacked in the City, Mr Herries and I moved it to Drummonds, 29 May.

June 8. Filed a bill against the Commercial Bank to compell them to give up their books and a copy of their letters to the agent at Coldstream in that shameful business; see 1828.

9. Investigated the extraordinary inquest at Ham Common on Mrs Palmer, and it was the most unsatisfactory inquiry I ever attended.

26. The Common Council agreed to address the King upon his escape at Ascott races *from a stone thrown*. I, with several aldermen, went and were as usual received upon the throne.

30. Attended the funeral of my much respected friend Captain Bird.

July 4. Went with a deputation of the Scots hospital to the King to congratulate him upon his escape at Ascott races[89]. Presented by the Duke of Buccleugh.

July 14. This day the freedom of the City was presented to Lord Grey and the other interested men who introduced the Reform Bill to ruin the tories and allow them to have the spoils, and a great dinner called the 'Reform dinner' was given in the Guildhall.

Cholera

The cholera raging and much fear existed in the minds of the people lest they should be the next victim to the dreadful malady. It raged in the prisons.

I was very unwell and no medicines relieved me. Had many invitations to public dinners. Resolved to go to Cheltenham to get rid of the invitations and after sending several apologies, left London on the 20 and slept at Oxford. Took Peter Laurie with me.

July 21. Went from Oxford to Cheltenham still very ill and sick. Remained a few days at Cheltenham still unwell and on the 26 went to Bath, the York House, the best and best conducted inn in England.

Went to Southampton on the 27, and read the account of my own death in the newspapers: 'That when a motion was expected to be brought before the magistrates of the county of Middlesex according to notice, Colonel Clitherow rose and said he had just been informed that Sir Peter Laurie had fallen a victim of the cholera.' My own immediate friends were well aware that allthough unwell I was or had gone to Cheltenham and I had fortunately written a letter from Bath to Lady Laurie.

I immediately wrote a letter and as the post was gone when I viewed the newspapers, I made up a parcel and sent it by the night coach, and on the following day a paragraph was sent to all the London newspapers, that I was still in the land of the living, but the many persons who sent to inquire how I was proved to me that I had many, many friends who were anxious about my welfare, and proved to my mind the advantage of having a good name. Having now been constantly sick for nearly a fortnight, I was at a loss what to do. All usual methods to get rid of the sickness was in vain. At last I thought of soda water and I took a glass which almost immediately removed my sickness.

We then sailed to Cowes[90] where we remained all Sunday[91]. We then went a tour through the island, I viewed the black gang choice, Shanklin, Ryde, Portsmouth, reached London the 3 August and received the usual welcome of my kind friends.

August 16. Set off for summer tour with Lady Laurie, Miss Wilkie, Peter Laurie and calaish, 3 horses. Slept at West Malling, Kent and on the 18th got to Sangate, went round the coast by Dover and reached Ramsgate on the 22, where we took a house 6½ guineas per week.

Election of Peter Laurie mayor

August 3. Came to London determined to remain in town to watch the Key or radical party and called everywhere and animated my friends. Pirie wrote to Pearson to know if he intended to oppose me. He said no, but as he always was a liar, I knew if he was paid for it he would do any dishonorable act. On the 12th Peter rode home in 2 days from Ramsgate to assist me. Attended Whiteday and made every preparation for a battle. Lady Laurie came home on the 20th. An opposition to me got up by Franks, they met at Guildhall coffee house on the 24th. Had all the watermen engaged by Dr Richardson. Went to the Stock Exchange. Well received everywhere.

September 29. Election of Mayor. On the 29 a placard was published reflecting on Key's friends, done no doubt to injure me, as I was accused of having published it. And before the election, after we came from church, Stevens came and asked me if I had published the placard, which I of course denied. I was unanimously elected Mayor, and although not allowed to address, or rather my friends were not allowed to address the hall in 1831, I was obliged to beg the Livery to hear Mr Stevens, Key's chairman. If I had been in London 1831 instead of trifling away my time at Brighton no opposition in 1831 would have shown its head and when it did, if I had not met with the painful accident, which laid me up for 6 weeks I should have then beat my opponents. Thus I close the brief account of my election by saying a man should always be upon the spot himself if he has any object to accomplish.

October 1. Attended the sheriffs at Westminster Hall and then dined with them at their hall, which was so hot that the windows were obliged to be broken to get air. My reception by the whole of the company was of the most gratifying description. I was then employed in ordering horses, carriages, liveries and maKing my preparation for a splendid show on the 9th November. Saw Mr Lamb, the under secretary of state and wished to know if the King would honor the City by dining at Guildhall on the 9th November. Mr Lamb congratulated me on my election and assured me that the government were glad to get rid of Key. They wanted a man of understanding and firmness, but I was much mortified to find from Mr Lamb when I called that the King had told Lord Melbourne that he considered the opening of London Bridge a visit to the City and would not come again.

23. Being very anxious to have a splendid show on the 9th I wrote to Colonel Lygon for the band of the Life Guards, which he politely refused. I then went to the adjutant general who said if I wrote to Lord Hill he would back my application. I did so and Lord Hill granted my request which was very gratifying as it was the first time the Life Guards' mounted band ever assisted in the Lord Mayor's pageant.

November 1. Had my presentation dinner *at the Albion* which was well attended. Had the Vice Chancellor and other private friends. Went to Brighton for a little peace, but caught a severe cold upon the roof of the coach.

6. Called upon and saw the Duke of Wellington and urged his grace to come to my dinner, but in vain. He said Thompson had said to the Privy council that his, the Duke's, presence would endanger the peace of the City and said emphatically that he would never dine again in the City.

8. A very wet day. Sat down to breakfast at ½ past 1 at the Mansion House. Was sworn in at 2 at Guildhall and was greatly cheered. Took the chair at the Mansion House, had 16 of my Company and 16 Stationers, Key's Company.

Lord Mayor's Day

November 9. Went and dressed in Woodthorpe's, had breakfast at 12, went in procession thro Smithfield, Aldersgate, Farrington Street, to the bridge. Got to Westminster at 2, reached Guildhall after being presented to the Chief Baron, Lyndhurst who made an ironical speech complimenting Key upon his second year, saying that none but great and astonishing men with wonderful abilities were assured at being a 2d time Lord Mayor. Had a most brilliant company, for particulars see newspapers. The account of the dinner is cut from the newspaper and pasted in scrap book. Got away ¼ before 12. Was greatly cheered in the streets in the whole line of procession and also much applauded at the dinner, no doubt from the recollection of my being ill used the year before. I endeavored to

make my friends and supporters happy. My speeches were bold and were well received, particularly when I said the Mansion House should be neutral ground.
10. Took my seat in the justice room, and told the officers that I intended during my year office that I required all their aid to clear London of the artful and experienced thieves, called the family and house breakers and forgers, and I was very successful as may be seen from the newspapers and my scrap book. As the stables were in a very dirty condition I resolved to remain in Park Square till they were cleaned and repaired, but went daily and did my own duty in the justice room[92].
16. The sheriffs joined with me and we gave the grandest ball that was given at the Guildhall and which cost nearly £1000. There were present 2600 persons. The company were all richly dressed, many of the aldermen and their families. This ball was greatly praised in the newspapers chiefly because it deserved it and also by employing Bleaden who puffs all the dinners he supplies.
20. The first Court of Aldermen. Sir Claudius Hunter proposed a vote of thanks to Key, the late Lord Mayor, which was not seconded.
26. The great reputation of our grand ball induced the committee of the Corporation schools to have a ball upon the same scale and about 1000 persons came. Tickets were 10/6, but no champayne or expensive wines.
28. This night slept for the first time in the Mansion House, having in the morning attended and opened the sessions, Guildhall.
29. A full state day, opened the sessions, Old Bailey, dined with the judges.
29. St Andrew's day. Having been requested to take the chair as the 2d Scots Lord Mayor, the stewards brought more friends than could comfortable dine in Bleaden's great room. The raptures and enthusiasm which every toast *I gave* or sentiment I uttered was quite overpowering, and it was one of the most painful, pleasing days I ever experienced when I considered the friendless state I came to London, with only my good spirits and industry to feed and clothe me[93]. The success which attended my exertions all this made it a very impressive day, and had such an effect upon me as made me languish and unwell for several days as nothing is so overwhelming to me as kindness and approbation.

Election of Marlebone

December 3. Parliament dissolved. The secretary of state wrote to me stating he wished all the elections to be on one day; having the arrangements of the City and the sheriffs, having to promote my interests in the boro of Marlebone, made me the returning officer. I assembled all the returning officers at the Mansion House on the 3d and we resolved to have the nomination, Saturday the 8th and the election on the 10th. Then rode to Portman barracks and ordered away all soldiers according to an order from the secretary of war.
6. This day I presided for the first time in the Common Council and made a speech which astonished the members. I stated that I should rather be considered a severe chairman than a negligent one, that I was determined firmly but

yet temporately to keep order. See papers.
7. Having appointed 8 deputies for 8 booths, I rode this day to see *all* the booths erecting and gave my orders respecting preserving the peace both in the City and Marlebone. As the sheriffs by the Reform Act were the returning officers for the City, they through the Common Cryer requested I would allow him to attend them with the mace. I consulted the Town Clerk and others and they agreed with me that the mace could only be where the Lord Mayor was and as I was not to be the mace must not.
8. Went to the chief booth, Portland Place and at 12 opened the meeting. I was so well received the people, that I told them I regretted I was not a candidate. The people were silent, *orderly* and well behaved and the nomination was over at 3. Murphy and Whalley had the show, Portman and Horne demanded a poll.
10. Attended the chief booth while Peto went into the City and voted for Lyall, then rode to the other booths.
11. Rode to all the booths, all going on very quiet.
12. Attended the chief booth. Opened the seals; Portman 4317, Horne 3320, Whalley 2165, Murphy 913, Jones 316. All over at 3, had a vote of thanks to Secretary Herald.
21. Attended my wardmote in full state. A poll was demanded; then Farrington, Waithman ill; then Queenhithe, Venables ill; then Portsoken, there being no alderman; a poll demanded. Had a vote of thanks at Farrington for having all the City and surburban elections in one day.
22. Attended contested elections in Aldersgate and Portsoker.

Messers Cole and Poynder from Bridewell and Bethlem hospitals called and said Sir R.C. Glyn had resigned. I well knew that they had an eye upon me, they having referred Sir Richard's resignation during the time Key was mayor, as it has generally been customary to elect the Lord Mayor as the president at any of the royal hospitals. But this is not always the case. During Key's years of office Lucas was chosen president of Bartholomew's.
24. Went and closed wardmote at Aldersgate, *Stacy chosen*, then to Portsoken. As I had noted against Scales it was supposed I should have been roughly treated; quite otherwise. Never did men behave better, never was I received better than by all the electors in a crowded church particularly from Scales and his immediate friends. A poll was demanded by Lyall, but at my earnest solicitation he abandoned it. Good humour and firmness carried me through.

I have thus recorded the leading incidents of the important to me year 1832, and although called a lord and everyone surpassing one another to pay me attention, I daily, hourly, sighed for Park Square and when I could be my own master, have a little leisure and not be as a mayor must be if he does his duty, a daily slave to the public and no applause, no approbation, and I had more than my share or more than I was entitled to, could compensate for the pleasure of independence.

1833

January 1. This day I opened for the first time the Boro Sessions in half state.
2. Dined black gown and North British. 44 dined.
4. The Common Council having voted a congratulatory address to Sir Thomas Denman. I went in half state with scarlet robe and about 20 of the aldermen and Common Council to his house, Russell Square, where the address was read by Common Seargent and a suitable answer from Denman. We took wine and cake.
7. Plowmonday. Had all the household to dinner, about 40.
9. Dined the Lord Mayor and sheriffs' committee and the Wardens and Court of Saddlers; 48.
15. According to custom after the first Court of Aldermen in the year all the aldermen and their ladies are invited. 21 aldermen and those who had ladies dined, the greatest number I ever saw at the Mansion House. In all with the City officers, 60 dined.

16. This was an important day to me, the election of president in the room of Sir R.C. Glyn. I had written a few letters to my friends and got that best of men, Mr Astell and Sir William Curtis, to propose and second me. When all were assembled and I had opened the business and retired, I was very nervous at having been kept so long in the committee room, when to my astonishment I found Mr Burgess had proposed the Duke of Sussex. I thought I had every chance of success, but it was fearful odds to be pitted against a royal duke. I expected a ballot[94] to be demanded. Mr Ramsbottom had the Duke's letter in his pocket accepting the election but seeing the feeling for me he withdrew the Duke's name and I was unanimously elected. This was one of the most gratifying days of my year and the finest pleasure in my life; see the newspapers. I was led in by Mr Astell and Sir W. Curtis and took my seat as the president, when I stated that during my year in the Mansion House I could attend but little but I would devote my time afterwards to the interest of the hospitals.
17. Fruiterers' Company and my own, Common Council dined 50.
21. The Saddlers' Company gave me a splendid dinner.
22. Attended dinner to celebrate Sir William Horne's election[95], and afterwards to a ball at Portsoken. A very hard frost. Lord Melbourne having agreed on behalf of His Majesty's ministers to dine with me and as an inducement said there should be no toasts to them he seemed delighted, and they all came and spent a pleasant evening. Sir James Shaw remarked after dinner that I was wrong in giving the King only, the (ministers) wished their healths drunk. When I mentioned this the Duke of Richmond said nothing was so rude as toasts. Lord Melbourne said he detested them. Lord Althorpe said when he had to speak after dinner he was in a funk all the time of dinner.
28. Attended the ball[96] to celebrate the return of Mr Portman at the Eyer Arms, the rooms crowded and many saying I must be the member first vacancy.
29. A splendid ball given me by the Saddlers.
31. Gave the first dinner to the Common Council, 50 attended.

February 6. This day Mr Alderman Waithman died. This I was much grieved at as he was a kind friendly man, a mere political actor in public and made the tool of a party, but at home he was a kind affectionate man, and was an excellent friend of mine. I served the office of *sheriff when he was* Lord Mayor, our friendship then commenced and was uninterupted until his death. This day gave the Bridewell fund £100.

13. A dinner to the Common Council, 39.

14. Attended Alderman Waithman's funeral with half state and second state liveries.

18. Went in full state to the election of an alderman in the room of Alderman Waithman. James Harmer was proposed, he was asked to pledge himself to all that was asked, he readily agreed to, and was elected a pledged slave instead of a free alderman.

25. This day being the Queen's birthday the Lady Mayoress and I went to the drawing room, was graciously received by their Majesties. In the evening dined with Lord Melburne; present the Lord Chancellor and all the judges. Sat down to dinner at ¼ before 8 and rose ¼ before 10. No toasts but 'Their Majesties'.

26. Court of Aldermen, Harmer sworn in and a Common Council dinner including Harmer's Common Council. 59 dined.

28. Another dinner at Common Council.

March 15. ditto ditto. Mr Portman having been harrassed out of his life by his new constituents in Marylebone resigned his seat in parliament and this the very day after I had again accepted[97] the office of returning officer. I was therefore, much to the disappointment of many, prevented being a candidate, but I was rather glad of it as I had no wish to slave for a metropolitan boro. I accordingly attended the hustings in Portland Place when Hope, Murray and Whalley were proposed. The election was on the following Monday, Tuesday and on Wednesday *20th* went to the hustings and declared Whaley the M.P.

April 4. As there were several repairs and painting wanted to 7 Park Square, I agreed to let Peter Laurie have all it could be let for and Messers Elgood and Ward let the house for 13 weeks at £20 per week.

8. The Ministers saying they could not dine on Easter Monday I put off my great dinner, but went to *Christ's* Church in full state, the Lady Mayoress with a pair, in private chariot. Copplestone gave us a lecture on political economy.

9. Easter Tuesday. I had appointed my own chaplain to preach the Spital sermon, his brother died and I was obliged to get Dr Russell who preached so good a sermon that the Court of Aldermen had it printed at the City expence.

10. A black gown dinner to which was added the directors of the North British and the directors of the Scots school society.

11. The Lady Mayoress, Miss Wilkie and myself were all taken very ill with the influenzy. I was kept to bedroom for 4 days and was 10 days ill[98].

17. Presided at a meeting of electors of London at Guildhall to petition the parliament to give poor laws to Ireland.

21. The antient custom of the judges dining after service at St Paul's on the first Sunday in Easter having been discontinued for two years, and finding it more agreeable to them to dine on the Sunday, although I never give or go to dinners on a Sunday, yet I was induced to give my dinner, and it was attended by the Lord Chancellor, Denman, and the other judges as is usual, but we had no toasts, but in all respects a quiet and sober dinner, all went away very early.

Having determined to try to get Sir Robert Peel and as many great men as possible from both the sides of politicks, I took great pains, and was greatly assisted by my excellent secretary Peter Laurie, and I believe never on any occasion was so many great men at one time under the roof of the Mansion House. The Marquis of Salisbury was as appeared to me, appointed by the tories to see the toasts, to know the names of those coming. All was arranged to my satisfaction, my trump card was Peel, and in maKing arrangements at the table, care was taken that he should sit near me, and the manner his health was received far exceeded my expectation. And such was the impression that the 'Times' accused me of packing the meeting with tories, and Mr Herries in the House of Commons also mentioned the reception of Peel at the Mansion House. Unfortunately the influenza kept some of the great people away, yet those that did come far, very far, exceeded any number of rank I ever saw at the Mansion House; see the 'Times' and 'Post', 25 April.

27. This day a great meeting was held at the Thatched House to promote a subscription to buy Abbotsford, attended by Peel, Malcom, Mahon and many great men. All our speeches were published in papers and afterwards in a pamphlet.

Sir George Murray having taken the chair at the Scots school society. I attended as Mayor, a guest meeting. George Laurie my cousin who left Scotland at an early period and settled with his brother in New York remained about 3 months in the Mansion House. He is a very gentlemany man, was much respected by all who met him and this day he saild from London to Scotland and after remaining there some time saild for New York.

May 1. This day took the chair for the lying-inn hospital, the Duke of Sussex on my right.

4. Of all the dinners in London the one where the greatest number are to be seen is the dinner at the Royal Academy. All the Whigs with Duke of Devonshire, Lord Grey at their head on the right of the chair, all the great tories on the left with the Duke of Wellington at their head. Sir M.Shee an excellent chairman. I was never so hot in my life, the room was crowded and badly ventilated.

11. Went to Southend, remained all Sunday, came up in a steam boat on the Monday but although it was the first time I had been absent, Lord Melbourne wrote on the Monday respecting the meeting in Spa Fields. A Lord Mayor is supposed to be always at home.

17. Bishops' dinner. This was one of the most splendid and best got banquets of the whole year. It was in the Hall, with flags etc etc. I invited the presidents of

all the S (blank) societies in London. The Duke of Somerset represented the Royal Institution, Sir H. Halford the Medical, Mr Wynne the Assiatic etc etc and about 19 bishops and several very distinguished persons, all well pleased, see newspapers.

18. This day I had a grand meeting in the Egyptian Hall to promote the Abbotsford subscription and many very distinguished speakers and nobles, see newspapers. The Marquis of Salisbury took the Chair when they voted me thanks, it was the first marquis, although many lords, such lords as soome of my predecessors, had been the president at the Mansion House.

28. King's birthday, went to drawing room, dined as before with Lord Melbourne, dined at 20, M(——)S. , rose from dinner ¼ past 9.

June 1. Heard from Scotland that my brother Alexander died 28 May.

3. The National schools examined at the Mansion House by the Bishop of London, dined afterwards at the London.

8. The Queen having agreed to attend St Paul's on the 13th to witness the children assembled, Peter wrote to Lord Denbigh to say when Her Majesty came into the City it was the duty of the Lord Mayor to meet her at Temple Bar to welcome her into the City and also begged she would condescend to come and partake of a cold collation at the Mansion House after service. I was gratified beyond measure when I had a letter saying she would come. I summoned a Court of Aldermen at the Mansion House on Monday at 10 o'clock. Two resolutions I had made that nothing could move me from my purpose of meeting the Queen at the Temple Bar, and that I would not consult the Common Council, not out of any disrespect to them but it would be the subject of such debate etc etc as would prevent the Queen coming.

13. A very wet morning. Went with the Lady Mayoress, 6 greys in half state carriage. Met the Queen and suite at Temple Bar. Conducted Her Majesty to her seat, grand sight. After service I went to the Mansion House and on the stairs met Her Majesty. A cold repast was set out in drawing rooms which the Queen, Duke of Gloster and Prince George with suite partook. The hall was fitted up with a throne, the Queen sat on the throne and the aldermen all in their robes marched in line from the bottom to the top of the hall making the salems on their way. I afterwards introduced all the aldermen and their ladies, City officers and their ladies, many of the *Saddlers' Company*, Common Councilmen and their ladies. The hall was fitted up with seats covered with scarlet, leaving the very large space in the middle for the ceremony, the Queen saluting the Lady Mayoress on the cheek according to Her Majesty's good will and pleasure. See newspapers.

14. A special Court of Aldermen and a vote of thanks for my conduct in receiving and entertaining the Queen.

18. A large party, private friends dined at the Mansion House.

20. Drawing room. The King asked about the water party, the Queen said she had been much gratified with her visit to the Mansion House[99].

'Resolved unanimously that the thanks of this court be given to the Right Honorable Peter Laurie, Lord Mayor, for having invited her most gracious Majesty the Queen to honor the Mansion House of this City with her royal presence after the anniversary meeting of the charity childern at St Paul's cathedral which Her Majesty had signified her intention to attend; for the prompt and effective measures taken in concert with his brother aldermen to receive Her Majesty at the enterance of the City with the respect and honor due to Her Majesty's exalted rank; and for the elegant hospitality with which Her Majesty was entertained by his Lordship during her visit at the Mansion House which will ever be recollected with the most lively feelings of respect. Woodthorpe.'

21. Held a Conservancy Court and dined at Greenwich, came home early and went to the Queen's ball, the grandest taking in the world. Supper at 1 o'clock saw many of the grandees I well knew, all very friendly.
24. Wilson and Harmer elected sheriffs without opposition.
18. Omitted the entered, the Common Council met and a friend of Key's, Gibbs, who always had hot suppers at the Mansion House brought a charge against me for using the word Corporation without calling the Common Council together[100]. Person seconded the motion, Legg asked if they had any charge against me, Pearson said no, only to record that the Corporation should not be used without the consent of Common Council. This gave me an opportunity of my presenting a copy of the proceedings respecting Queen's visit, and thus it came upon the minutes of the Common Council. I had about 50 neatly bound and sent them to the King, Queen, all the royal family and the Saddlers and many private friends. Thus that which was intended a censure turned out much in my favor and thus terminated one of the most gratifying events in my life. Never, never shall I forget the Queen's visit to the Mansion House, 13 June 1834 (actually 1833).
26. A precept was issued for the election of alderman for Portsoken in the room of Hughes who had not defended his election. I was told I should be murdered by the Butchers as I had been active against Scales. I took *D.* Pollock as my assessor and to my great astonishment the people were as friendly to me as before. A poll demanded and begun.
27. Sons of the clergy went to St Paul's in full state at 2, got away at *½ past* 5. A heavy service, too much of a good thing, music. Went in the evening to Lambeth Palace, the most extravagant dinner I ever saw but very, very splendid. The 2 footmen that ushered in the company and waited upon the Archbishop had full court dresses with bag wigs and swords. Present Sussex, Sir Robert Peel etc etc. All very grand, no toasts but the King, Sussex and archbishop.
28. Attended the close of the poll at Portsoken; Scales 155, Johnson 70. I put in Pollock's return that the election had fallen on M. Scales esq. I had a strong vote of thanks for my conduct as a magistrate, for entertaining the Queen at my own

expence and for my conduct in presiding over the election.
29. Presented a piece of plate to Samuel Dixon and read a written address, written by Peter which was very good and greatly applauded. Dixon felt it much, all parties gratified. The reporter did not insert the address. Mr Dixon called *upon me*, said if the address was not to be published[101] he cared not if the plate was thrown into the Thames. I sent it to the newspapers and it was inserted.
30. This day a sermon[102] was preached, a sermon for the Highland schools at St Ann's, Westminster. I did that which was very bold, I went in state and took the sword and mace into Westminster, out of the City jurisdiction, but it was for a charitable purpose and we had a splendid sermon and a large collection.
July 3. This day gave a grand entertainment to Sir Hussey Vivian, Sir Edward Kerrison, Sir Frances Freeling, Lord Paumare, Clitherow, Coast etc etc. The entertainment was in the hall with flags and the same as the bishops' dinner.
5. This day was the anniversary festival at Bridewell, and the first time of my presiding at president, about 134 dined, what was *said was well* received. This is a very comfortable dinner, all the luxuries of the season, with turtle, dine at 5 and all away before 9.
8. The Duke of Buccleuch's party put off in consequence of the rain.
12. The public journals alone are equal to the task of describing the Duke of Buccleuch's party. The King and Queen and cortege were received suitable to the ranks of the parties, public spirit and wealth of the Duke. The day was fine. The King and Queen sat up(on) sofas placed in the lawn, where we had boat races and the immense company, the river covered with boats, the lawn crowded with all the nobility and wealth and rank in the county dressed like princes. At 6 o'clock the tents which were pitched on all parts of the ground were opened to the public. I never saw such a scramble. I found the lords and ladies were as anxious for the good things of this world as citizens and could push as hard to obtain them. Came away ½ past 10, was 2 hours in trying to get carriage up but was at last obliged to walk a mile to get at it.
13. Went to Hertford and returned on Sunday after seeing a boy I had placed in the Blue Coat School.
17. Had a letter stateing that my sister Mrs Gray had died, aged 68, a better woman never lived.
18. This was my grand water party, for description see court journal, and for the rank see the invitation book. All very happy and much delighted with one of the most delightful and gratifying sights connected with the City, to see well dressed company dancing on deck in daylight, viewing the banks of the beautiful Thames.
20. Dined with Navigation, drove to Pope's villa, went through the house, took Lady Laurie and Miss Wilkie[103].
22. Dined with Wax Chandlers, Blackwall, upon the invitation of Alderman Cowan, a large party.

23. Took the chair at Mr Warden's meeting to assist in making him a director of the East India Company, a good meeting.
24. Conservancy. Went with 4 greys and out-rider to Stratford, then crossed the river to Greenwich where we dined. Had several friends particularly the Lord Provost of Edinburgh.
25. A severe contest for Common Sergeant, Law having been elected Recorder. Mirehouse 125, Hill 110. The only vote I gave during my year of office was for Mirehouse to keep out the radical.
27. Dined with Alderman Wilson, Beckenham.
30. Dined with Mr Anderton's annual party at Blackwall, 40 dined, several M.P.s but nearly all radicals.
31. City Lands up the river took Lady Laurie to Miss Wilkie's, then drove to Richmond, drove up towing[104] path and got in in the middle of the river.
August 1. A Common Council at 1 o'clock over at 3.
3. Went to Tunbridge Wells incognito to look for a house or lodging for the Lady Mayoress for a few weeks. On the coachbox a fellow called the coachman, smoked cigars all the way to my great annoyance as I sat outside. After remaining all the Sunday at this delightful place, and returned on Monday.
5. Dined at the Drapers'. While at dinner Mr Whittle Harvey sent a letter saying that Key had resigned his seat in Parliament to prevent an enquiry into his disgraceful conduct, disgraceful in every respect. He is a disgrace to the aldermen and to human nature, a convicted liar and a base and unworthy fellow. Had serious thoughts of standing for the City.
7. Finding that Kemble still persevered in his intention of standing for the City although Lyall's committee refused to support him I, rather than divide the conservative interest, declined standing and sent notes to Mr Kemble and my friends to that effect.

Fancy fair for foreigners in distress. The Queen having asked me at *at the Duke of Buccleuch's* to allow a fancy fair to dispose of the remainder of the stock which had not been disposed off at Hanover Square rooms, I cheerfully complied[105] and the Mansion House was fitted up accordingly. The fair lasted 2 days and was fashionably attended and was very productive. 1400 persons attended and paid 1/-. All the Corporation did not attend. Wrote to the Honorable George Lamb enclosing a letter to Lord Melbourne respecting the Queen's visit.
10. Lady Laurie and Miss Wilkie with the chariot, coachman and one footman set off for Tunbridge Wells *and Eastbourne* for a few weeks. This day the Corporation appointed to give the medical officers a piece of plate each for their exertions in devoting their time and skills to caring and removing the dreadful desease called *the* cholera morbus[106]. Pearson in the chair, supported Marquis of Lansdown and Lord Ackerman. I, with a speech, presented pieces of silver worth (blank) each to Drs Babington, Roupell, Ridout, Field and Degrave. A very pleasant evening, all went off well.

14. Saddlers' Hall. Attended church with sword and mace, heard a sermon from Mr Gibson, after we returned to Saddlers' Hall, I was elected Master of the Company it being my regular turn to be master, but as there was a special session at the Old Bailey to rectify the mistakes at the Clerkenwell sessions, I was obliged to dine at the Old Bailey with the judges.
16. W. Crawford having agreed to oppose Kemble, two Courts of Aldermen were called to make him free of the City, but we could not make a Court. At last a Court of Common Council was called and we made a Court of Alerman and Crawford was sworn in.
17. Peter and John went in a tilbury and spent *Saturday evening and* Sunday at Staines, Windsor Park, etc, and returned on Monday morning.
22. The directors of the North British gave me a dinner.
23. Appointed Alderman Brown locum tenens.
24. D.Wilkie and I went by coach to Eastbourne to see Lady Laurie and Miss Wilkie, remained there all Sunday, drove to Pevensay castle and returned on the Monday.
31. Savory's case, Mansion House.
September 3. The coachman having come from Hastings to drive the state coach, proclaiming Bartholemew fair and this day that abominell nuisance was allowed and proclaimed by the usual people.
4. Black gown dinner, 45 dined.
5. Mr Wooller said to me that Joseph Ady promised that after my year of office he would plague me.
7. Peter went to meet Lady Laurie and Miss Wilkie at Hastings.
8. Went to two City churches, no congregation. The City churches I have visited, 21 have no congregations, the half of them ought to be pulled down and others united.
12. Saddlers' feast and ball which I attended.
13. Went with Herring to Burbridge's horticutral fete, which Porter puffed in the 'Morning Post'. It was well got up and well attended.
14. Watford. D. Wilkie, Peter and John went in tilbury and saddle horse to Watford, Essex Arms. Went on the Sunday heard the Honorable Reverend Mr Capel and I remarked it was religion made easy. Drove over to Castlebury park and came home on Monday morning.
16. Attended Scots School society, Freemasons at 7 and agreed to send £1000 to Scotland.
17. Lady Laurie and Miss Wilkie returned from their summer tour of Tunbridge Wells, Eastbourne and Hastings.
19. Was sworn in as master Saddlers' Company and dined with the Company.
21. A state day: went to Christ's Hospital, sermon preached by Mr Dolling at St Botolph's, Aldersgate, their own church repairing, and heard afterwards the 2 Grecians. Dined with the governors, Poynder in the chair.

24. Having stated that I would give the ladies of the Saddlers' Company a ball when I was mayor at the Mansion House and having given with the sheriffs a ball at the Guildhall and invited all the Saddlers' ladies, still they were not satisfied and I accordingly gave them a splendid ball at the Mansion House, a supper which I contracted for at 5/- a head including tea and coffee but not wine.
25. Had two heavy days in the justice room respecting British leaf tea which occupied 4 hours each day and created a great contend. I was determined to condemn the tea, the City Solicitor at first was against me, but at last he, Mr Hobbs, agreed with me and we condemned the tea to be burnt, and I was threatened with a law suit. The solicitor for the Excise asked wether I would be defended by him or the City and said him. Proceedings were taken, but the case never was heard nor trial attempted.

Went with William in tilbury to Staines where we slept, a good inn. Went to meet the Newgate committee to view the City boundaries. The barge came up after breakfast, we then went to the stone and after we walked 3 times round the stone I knocked (off) the neck of a bottle of wine. The committee took theirs out of glasses, I out of the broken bottle and after drinking prosperity to the City of London, honest men, and pretty women of Staines with 9 times 9, we embarked in the shallop had a delightful sail down the river, had turtle etc, Tickner chairman, and arrived at Queenhithe about 9 o'clock.
27. A deputation consisting of Mr Williams and Mr Nicholson called upon me to ask me to serve a second year, which after thanking them gratefully I stated my health would not allow me, *and my respect of the rotation* and I pointedly declined.
28. This day Mr Alderman Farebrother was elected Lord Mayor. Previous to the election he was asked if he would call Common Council and Halls when requested and upon that declaration was not opposed. After the election was over and conducted as usual, Mr Nicholson came forward and proposed a vote of thanks to me and dwelt upon my great merits in having rooted out theives etc etc. This was seconded by Mr Matthews. Mr Hunt objected to that part of my conduct respecting spurious tea, I replied that if it had been roasted coffee I should act *in* the same way, which turned the laugh upon Mr Hunt and my vote was carried unanimously as follows:

Laurie, Mayor. In a meeting or assembly of the Mayor, Aldermen and Liverymen of the several Companies of the City of London in Common Hall assembled at the Guildhall of the sacred City on Saturday 28 September 1833.

'Resolved unanimously that the thanks of this Common Hall be given to the Right Honorable Sir Peter Laurie, Lord Mayor, for having discharged the arduous and important duties of his high station with a zeal, ability and impartiality which has never been surpassed, for the punctuality, vigilance and discrimination displayed by him in the daily administration of public justice to which, amongst other beneficial results the public are indebted for the exposure of and vertual annihilation of a system of swindling and depredation carried on with impunity for a long period and to an unprecedented extent, and above all for his ready acquiescence at all times with the wishes of the citizens and electors of London in convening meetings for the expression of their sentiments, and for his uniform courtesy and strict impartiality when presiding over their deliberations. Woodthorpe.'

I never knew anyone who had a more gratifying reception than I had and particularly from those who were politically opposed to me. I took the Lord Mayor elect home with me in the state carriage and entertained all the aldermen and City officers at the Mansion House[107].

30. This day we proceeded as usual to the Court of the Exchequer and presented the new sheriffs, Aldermen Wilson and Harmer, when the usual fulsome compliments were paid the new sheriffs, and the congratulatory address to the old sheriffs, Humphrey and Peck. We afterwards had what is called the sheriffs' dinner at the London Tavern, the company was numerous but not the first rate merchants, indeed fewer men of rank than I ever saw on a similar occasion. All went off well and I was in good spirits in the chair. I thus parted with two sheriffs with whom I had been associated during the whole year, and I found them obliging, kind, unobtruding and just the persons likely to make a Lord Mayor comfortable as far as the office of sheriff is concerned. Humphrey gave two or three good dinners, Peck gave none.

The 'Standard' newspaper of this day gave a long leading in my favor as a magistrate and nothing could be more complementary. The concluding, 'Sir Peter's popularity, for popular he is in the best sense, is wholly unconnected with politicks or party. He is popular because he has steadily, ably and with good humour discharged the important duties of his office. This is the conservative style of earning popularity, for conservative we are proud to say, Sir Peter is'. Hae tibi erunt artes ('These be thine arts.' Virgil, *Aeneid*, VI, 852).

October 1. The 'True Sun' in a leading article refers to me says:

'We have upon more than one occasion borne a willing, grateful testimony to the really excellent, and we may almost say unexceptional, conduct of Sir Peter Laurie in his capacity as chief magistrate. We more particularly expressed upon some short time since the sense we entertained of his high and rare merits as a magistrate, we did so in terms as warm as our respect, for his magisterial character is sincere. While our contemporaries, whig, tory and radical, the "Chronicle", "Standard" and "Examiner", are expressing themselves to the same effect, we will not deny ourselves the pleasure of offering our congratulations of opinion which prevails respecting the manner in which he has discharged his functions as chief magistrate, on the high and just estimations in which his services are held by all classes of this fellow citizens, unanimity in this is as wonderful as stage unanimity. It's seldom indeed that all parties can agree in praising and still more seldom that they can with justice so slightly qualified as that which Sir Peter Laurie's good sense, fine moral courage and strict impartiality are now being rewarded.'

After commenting upon, the 'Standard' says:

'Most certainly as our contemporary says, Sir Peter is not popular on account of his politics, but we admit him to be popular and deservedly so in spite of them. We quite concur with a large body of our fellow citizens in wishing this able magistrate could have been prevailed upon to serve, allow himself to be put *a second time* in nomination for the office which he is shortly to retire from. We are thankful however for his one year of good service and hope his successor may profit by his example'.

'Examiner' says men of all parties concur in the approbation of Sir Peter Laurie as chief magistrate. The tribute to his merit is carried by acclamation. It is generally agreed that so efficient a magistrate never before filled the civic chair etc etc. All the other newspapers put in leaders, except the 'Times', a thing very unusual, unexpected by me, therefore the more gratifying. But the 'Times' amply made up for this in their complimentary articles, 1835.

11. Tea case concluded. This day was appointed to decide the important case of British leaf; was argued from 11 to 4, when with the concurrence of the City Solicitor I condemned the leaf to be burnt, notice was served upon me to bring an action against me, I agreed that the Excise should defend me but it soon was abandoned.

22. This day the City Solicitor *and Peter* and I went to Gravesend to view the *intended* peir and then heard all that could be said for and against the temporary peir having been put up. After a quiet dinner and speaking kindly to the honest watermen, they were so pleased that when we came out they took the horses from the carriage and drew us out of the town, a proof in my mind that the lower classes, when treated kindly, will always prove grateful.

24. See an article on the judges and the Lord Mayor.

29. The Court of Aldermen rejected unanimously Scales and elected or appointed *Johnson to be* alderman.

November 1. Common Council was occupied this day in considering an article in the 'Chronicle' stating the extravagant conduct of the Lord Mayor's committee, my committee. Suspicion was awakened that Peter Laurie wrote it. I stated that my expenditure would be about £11,500 being (£)4,000 more than I received. The 'Chronicle' very honestly refused to give up the author of the article. article.

5. This was a most gratifying day to me[108]. My friends resolved to give me a piece of plate worth 200 guineas. It was got up amongst them in a very few days

and the subscriptions entered into and this day was appointed to present the plate to me and at the same time to give me a dinner, about 50 gentlemen met at the dinner given at the Albion. Mr Easthope in the chair. Not a member of the Corporation was asked, it was my own ward and private friends, amongst whom were all the directors of North British Life Office. An excellent account was given by all the newspapers in the 6th November and it was a day I can never forget nor the kindness of my friends, it was got up in a great hurry that it might be given to me before I left the office. The peice of plate is very handsome and a complementary inscription is on the plate, and afterwards was added a pedestal of the old oak which had been used as piles in the old London Bridge and had been 700 years under water is neatly mounted with silver with the City vote of thanks and other ornaments.

9. The proceedings of this day[109] is given in the newspapers. There was no novelty in them except the very flattering encomium passed upon me by Lord Lyndhurst which was with a drawing of the piece of plate and the Recorder's speech, letter printed and sent, maliciously sent, by D. Richardson to each of the aldermen, which did not give I think entire satisfaction as they neither had plate nor such a speech from the Chief Baron. I was much cheered by the mob in the street, a very unusual reception for one who is not supposed to be opposed to the existing government, for the populace are generally opposed to all governments and loudly cheer those who are hostile to government. All the minsters were present but Grey, the greatest applause was given to the Queen's health and the Duke of Wellington. As Mr Farebrother wish to take possession of the Mansion House on the very first day, I gave him possession and we slept in 7, Park Square, rejoiced to get back to our own quiet abode. Never did anyone quit the Mansion House with more pleasure than I did I had not one day's good health or comfort while in it.

14. Started for Brighton with 4 horses, 2 saddle and 2 carriage. Slept at Red Hill. Party consisted of Lady Laurie, Peter and coachman and groom. Hunted daily and remained at the Albion till 23, then took a house, 78, King's Road.

December 2. Came in the stage coach at 12 and dined club.

3. This being the first Court of Alderman after I had quitted the civic chair it was as usual the day for giving me a vote of thanks as it generally is a mere matter of form. I was however detained in Mr Temple's office for an hour while they were debating upon my vote of thanks, for the two lawyers, Messers Brown and Harmer did not approve of my mode of examining prisoners, as it was not the usual mode, which is to tell prisoners not to criminate themselves and rest[110] like nonsense. The vote was as follows:

Court of Aldermen. Farebrother Mayor.

'Resolved unanimously that the thanks of this court be presented to the Right Honourable Sir Peter Laurie, knight, late Lord Mayor of this city, for the courtesy which has marked his conduct in presiding over this court, for the urbanity displayed at all times in his intercourse with his colleagues in the magistrcy and all classes of his fellow citizens and for the hospitality with which he has sustained the ancient dignity of his important office and that, while this court cannot concur in the principles upon which the late Lord Mayor has acted in his examination of prisoners brought before him upon criminal charges, they have great pleasure in recording their opinion that in all such proceedings his lordship has acted in the exercise of an honest, though in the opinion of this court, a mistaken judgement. Woodthorpe.'

4. Called at the Town Clerk's and saw the deputy Lorkin with the vote of thanks, proposed as I thought by the Town Clerk, nothing could be better.
5. Attended Common Council and waited in the Court of Aldermen to know the issue of any vote of thanks when Mr Lorkin and Mr Walton came and said Mr Gibbs would vote against my vote unless the Queen's visit to the Mansion House was omitted. I said I would sooner divide the court, but only two hands, Mr Gibbs and Mr Prior held up against it and the vote was as follows.

Farebrother Mayor.
'That the thanks of this court be presented to the Right Honorable Sir Peter Laurie, knight, late Lord Mayor, for the punctuality, diligence, and attention with which he has discharged the various and important duties attached to that arduous office during the past year, for the eminent services he has rendered to the public by his activity and perseverance in the investigation of many difficult cases, whereby several notorious dilinquents have been brought to punishment and the public secured against the continuance of their depredations, for the countenance and support he has given to the various benovelent institutions of this metroplis for the relief and education of the poor, for the anxiety he has evinced in the maintenance of the dignity and hospitality of this City, particularly on the occasion of her Majesty's, the Queen's visit on the anniversary of the charity children at St Paul's cathedral, for the urbanity of his manners and the ready access he has at all times afforded to the members of this court and his fellow citizens, for the promptitude with which he's complied with their wishes in convening this court and on other public meetings and for the impartiality with which he has presided over them. Woodthorpe.'

Resolved that the above be framed and glazed and presented to the late Lord Mayor and be advertised in all the papers.

Went in the afternoon to Brighton.
6. This day the advertisement appeared of my vote of thanks from the Court of Aldermen and I wrote a letter addressed to the town clerk and sent a copy to all the morning papers:

Brighton. 6th December 1833.
My dear sir, I observe by an advertisement in the daily paper that the Court of Aldermen have done me the honor of voting me three thanks for my humble services during my mayoralty. While I accept *this* with great gratification as a proof of the cordial feeling existing between my colleagues and myself, I cannot but express[111] some surprise that without the usual previous intimation, in my absence and with closed doors the opportunity should have been taken of appending to the vote a sort of protest reflecting on my mode of examining prisoners. I can refer with pride to the course I have pursued which have been acknowledged by the livery of London and the Common Council in their highly flattering vote of yesterday. My only anxiety has been to convict the guilty and release the inmates as speedily as possible. I have never pressed a prisoner for an answer but I have prevented attornies interfering to keep back information which might be beneficial to the prisoners by terminating the case at once without subjecting him to the odium and expense of a trial at the Old Bailey. My services are before the public and I feel if there had been much real cause of complaint they would have been as prompt to censure as they have been kind in approving. I have frequently acknowledged my obligations to my colleagues for their friendly advice and assistance but feeling the soundness and propriety of the maxim "inter pares non est potestas" (between equals there is no authority) and that no magistrate has the slightest authority to animadvert on the judicial conduct of a colleague, I beg with the utmost good feeling towards my excellent friends to protest against these unusual and irregular criticism though I have much pleasure in expressing my opinion that it was done in the exercise of an honest though mistaken judgement.
Your servant, Peter Laurie.

The 'Chronicle' says:

'Sir Peter Laurie in his answer[112] to address of the Court of Aldermen which our readers will find in another column expresses himself with becoming spirit at the insidious manner in which his brethren availed themselves of the pretext for voting him thanks to impeach his conduct in the exercise of his judicial duties at a time when he was not present to defend himself. Sir Peter may rest assured the motives of his brethren may injure themselves but cannot injure him. We predicted that Sir Peter would have no sucessor he had the good of the public only in view.'

The 'Examiner' is still stronger in praising my system, as it was called. Remained hunting till the 18th December when we all returned to town. The 'Herald' attacked my system, which Peter Laurie replied dated 7 December and published, 'Herald', 13 December.

21. A wardmote Aldergate and a 3 days poll as usual. Closed 24, the old members chosen.

1834.

January 2. Dined Middlesex magistrates and qualified Peter Laurie for the table.

7. Attended Court of Aldermen. Copeland asked me if I acknowledged the letter published 6 December, which I did. He moved that the letter should be considered, no seconder and not a word said upon the subject.

21. Aldermen's dinner 12 attended.

February 7. This day prevented the house from being robbed. Lady Laurie and Miss Wilkie and Peter went to a ball, Mansion House. I went to Royal Institution and came home and found a thief in the house let in by the footman, Walter Taylor, who did not expect me till 1, and I came home at 11. Took them both to the watchhouse. Pettigrew ageed to give for me £100 pounds to Phillips to paint a bishop's length[113].

10. Sat to Phillips first time. The Lord Mayor, Farebrother, refused to lend me the entertaining gown, but the Vice Chancellor, Shadwell, kindly lent me his which is the same as the Lord Mayor's, and Woodthorpe lent me an excellent drawing of the collar and jewell.

April 1. Faulkner agreed for Peter Laurie to hold briefs for Perkins, Smithfield market. The builders Hutchins and Stephens who erected the hustings for the Marlebone election agreed to be content with the sum I received. I took £50 for Murphy instead of £75, they were then over paid but they brought an action against me and I, rather than go to court, paid the £25. Cost in all about £70. Owing to the roguery of C. Richards and J. Thompson, threw up my appointment of returning officer.

May 9. The Queen came to the 'Sons of the Clergy' and paid me such marked attention the honorary treasurer gave me the £50. This gave such grave offence that the Lord Mayor brought the subject before the Court of Aldermen.

10. Drove to Hatfield and slept.

11. Drove to Hertford, went to Quaker's meeting and church. Saw James Reed and came home afternoon.

28. Went to King's drawing room, then dined Aldersgate. Deputy John Smith in the chair. Got Sir C. Flower to resign and went to Pirie who was elected in this seat.

June 4. Congratulated Pirie on his election.

6. Colonel Clitherow, Mr Cole, Mr William Cole and Poynder left Bridewell at 9 o'clock in a landaw and 4 horses, went thro Barnett, Hatfield and slept Peterboro.

7. Left Peterboro at 8, got to Wainfleet at 2. Went to several farmers and got back to dinner at 7. Mr Hardwick joined us.

8. Went to church in landaw, heard a good preacher Mr Latton, then went to a

decoy and saw the manner they take wild ducks.
9. Drove and looked at the farms, bad roads.
10. Left Wainfleet and got to Eaton where we slept.
11. Started at 9 and got to London ½ past 3 after a delightful tour and very fine weather, made the tenants very happy.
11. Pirie sworn in Court of Aldermen.
14. Dined Clitherow.
24. Raphael, a catholic, and Illidge chosen sheriffs.
July 4. The annual dinner Bridewell, 150 dined.
5. Went to Woolwich and saw the Queen depart for Germany.
9. John Laurie married Miss Eliza Collett. We all went to the wedding breakfast and dined afterwards at Mrs Collett, a very expensive dinner.
17. Colonel Clitherow, 2 Coles and self went in an open small caleche, went to Star, Oxford, had a cold dinner, Henley at 5. The hottest day I ever felt in England. Mr Hardwick joined in the evening. Many horses died.
18. Set off at 10 to Northleah, viewed the farms, Blenham, and returned and dined Oxford to dinner. A very wet day.
19. Left Oxford 10 o'clock, got to London ½ past 4.
27. Sent 4 horses to Rickmansworth, Mr Ardens.
28. Left London for Rome etc, the party consisting of Lady Laurie, Miss Wilkie, Peter and self with a landaw hired for 4 or 8 weeks. Slept at the York, Dover.
29. Calais and then to St Omer where we slept.
30. Cassells. 31. Towrnay. **August** 1. Brussells. 4. Lovain. 5. Luge. 6. Aix la Chappel. 8. Cologne. 9. Bonn. 10. Andernach. 11. St Goar. 12. St Goar. 13. Wiesbaden. Intensely hot.
15. Frankfurt; on the way to Franfort at Hattersheim met the Queen of England who was as usual very condescending and kind, as was all her suite.
25. Darmstadt. 26. Bruschell. 27. Baden Baden. 30. Strasbourg. 31. Kohl. **September** 1. Friburgh. 2. Bondorf. 3. Shaffhausen. Intensely hot. 5. Lensburg. 6. St Michael. 7. Bern. 9. Pyrnne. 10. Lausanne. 11. Geneva. 18. Marez. 19. Poliquy. 20. Dijon. 22. Tonnerre. 23. Lens. 24. Fountainbleau.
25. Paris, remained in Paris till 10 October.
October 10. Vernon. 11. Rouen. 13. Dieppe. 14. Abbeville. 15. Bologne. 19. Calais. 20. Dover; nearly dead, dreadful passage. 21. London.
23. Attended Middlesex magistrates and made a speech to let everyone know I had returned and that I was much happier in England than seeing all the strange sights with all the inconvenience of travelling with a bad stomach, at least one which required the greatest care.
24. Had my 4 horses from grass and hired new servants and settled at home for the winter, putting our house in order *not* to lease it but to reside in it.
November 1. This day was opened the central criminal court, 12 judges present with Lord Chancellor Brougham. This court, if I have not said so before in this memorandum book, was brought about by my nephew and myself, with

Sir Frederick Roe. When the magistrates of Middlesex began to hold intermediate sessions we wished intermediate sessions at the Old Bailey, legal difficulties occurred, at last a draught of a Bill was found in Mr Clark's office' drawer by his uncle Mr Shelton and Recorder Sylvester, which was adopted at the Home Office and carried through the Lords etc by Brougham. The judges afterwards dined with the Lord Mayor, Farebrother, but as I said I never would dine[114] at the Mansion House during the remainder of his year I declined going to the dinner.
3. This day Lord Mayor elect Winchester was presented to the Lord Chancellor, *Brougham*, Lincoln's Hall. I afterwards dined with him at the Albion, the presentation dinner.
6. Mr Phillips not having been successful in painting my portrait, agreed to paint me again and I began the horrid torture of sitting.
10. Dined on the Lord Mayor's Day, all the cerimonials as usual.
11. Saw Lords Melbourne, Duncannon, etc upon the defective *Act of* weights and measures, and relieved them much by stating that I would at the next county day render the Act null and void by recommending the magistrates to fine those who had not got their weights stampt one farthing, and I did so.

Peter Laurie wrote an able article to the 'Times' inserted as a leading article stating who were the *real* authors of the Criminal Court Bill.
15. Change of Ministers. Duke of Wellington sent for and he took upon himself all the principal offices of the state until the return of Sir Robert Peel, which seemed to give great satisfaction to the country.
19. The Middlesex magistrates for the first time invited the sheriffs, Raphael and Illidge, that they might invite the chairman, this was supposed.
25. Court of Aldermen decided upon opening the Court, motion by Copeland, 10 to 10. Lord Mayor Winchester gave the casting vote against opening.
December 1. Duke of Gloster died. Dined with the Scots Hospital, St Andrew's day falling on a Sunday. Sir G. Murray in the chair. The Common Council went up with an address to the King complaining of his dismissal of his ministers, which address was carried by a small majority on the 27. Only one alderman, Harmer, went up with the address. Peter Laurie wrote in the 'Times' an able letter signed 'Spectator against the dismissal of parliament'[115].
6. This day I received a most gratifying letter from the Duke of Buccleuch, stating that I was so popular in Scotland that he and his conservative friends were desirous of starting me for the Haddington district of Burghs, that Jedburgh was secured etc and refered me to Sir F. Drummond and D. Horne esq. I replied I was not anxious to stand *or to have a seat in Parliament*,. but if they thought I was almost certain I would allow my name to be given.
11. Wrote to D. Horne, Edinburgh, that I had given up all thoughts of Haddington as the desision was to be immediate.
17. Received a letter from Sir F. Drummond saying we had employed agents in the 5 Burghs. I answered refering to my letter to D. Horne and still declining.

18. Rode to Dr Morison and asked him to write to Mr Brown, Provost of Haddington, a confidential letter to learn if I had any chance as the parties were so urgent for my coming to Scotland.
20. Was sent for to Peel's where I saw letters from Scotland urging my immediate departure. I resolved to send my nephew, went home from Peel's, wrote my address with the assistance of Peter Laurie, sent them off by post to be printed and circulated in Haddington, Jedburgh and Dunbar and that my nephew would go off immediately.
21. Peter Laurie went off by the York coach at 8 o'clock to canvass the Burghs.
22. An excellent article in 'Morning Post' respecting Haddington.
22. Held a wardmote, a poll demanded.
23. The great dinner given to Peel and Wellington, at the Mansion, excellent speakers. I was by everyone congratulated upon my certain success of getting the Haddington Burghs. A splendid day.
24. Ward election over. Old members elected.
25. Saw Provost Brown's salty reply to D. Morison and found him to be a canting, hypocritical radical and a voluntary churchman. He enclosed an address to Steuart. 120 names. I then saw I had no chance, still I would give Peter Laurie the opportunity and wrote to Lord Dalhousie, Houston, *Dr.* Lee and Aitchison. Had also a letter from Jedburgh, not favorable.
27. Had a very sensible letter from Peter Laurie from Dunbar, stating that the Burghs were gone, that we were too late in the field, that they were all radicals and mad. Called and told Sir R. Peel's private secretaries.
31. The 'Courier' stated that Peter Laurie had gone on a wild goose[116] errant to the Burghs. This I believe ended my prospect or even desire to be M.P. for any part of my native land. The Reform Bill has been in my opinion the ruin of the respectabity of the members and voters for Scotland. Had most pleasing letters from Lord Lauderdale, the Marquis of Tweedale and Lord Dalhousie, that later nobleman kindly offered me his mansion at Coulston to remain there as long as I pleased. This was the more pleasing as I was born upon the Coulston estate.

1835

January 1. Signed an address to Sir Robert Peel.
2. Joined Wood's committee at Charing Cross, candidate for Middlesex.
3. Peter returned by Liverpool etc from the Haddington Burghs after dining with Proffessor Wilson etc.
5. Nomination City election. Radicals had the shew by a large majority.
6. Voted for Wood, Lyall, Ward and Wilson but I had stated to Mr Buckle on the 4 that nothing could be so improper as starting Ward and Wilson, that by so doing we should lose Lyall, and it was so.
12. Went to the nomination Middlesex election at Brentford, went upon the hustings and made a speech in favor of Thomas Wood which was greatly praised. In 'Times' a good report.

19. Went to Brentford where Byng and Hume were declared duly elected. I spoke in proposing a vote of thanks to[117] the sheriffs. A cuting speech.
20. The aldermen's dinner at the Mansion House, a good muster.
29. Attended a Conservative dinner at Hampstead. I spoke in favor of the good cause but was very ill all night.
30. Bought a horse.
February. Ansley removed to Bridge ward and Lainson elected in his stead.
7. Joseph Ady having assumed the name of James Laurie and having obtained money from the notion that I had a brother of that name, I was examined as a witness at the Old Bailey when Ady was tried for the offence of obtaining money under false pretences and sentenced to 7 years' transportation afterwards remitted to one year's imprisonment.
13. Having my picture painted by Mr Halls when I was sheriff I had the collar of the mayor painted upon the picture and altered for the Lord Mayor with new frame, and presented[118] it to the Saddlers for their Hall. They then summoned a special Court to received the same.
15. Mr Birnie my old friend and most intimate friend of Lady Laurie's family died. He was an excellent man. This is a great error, he was a worthless man. P.L. 1849[119].
19. The new House of Commons met when Mr Abercrombie was proposed as speaker by Lord J. Russell and had votes 316, Sutton 306, Abercrombie's majority, 10.
24. A special Court of Saddlers to receive my portrait in due form, when a vote of thanks highly complementary was unanimously carried and ordered to be framed and glazed. The following is the vote of thanks (page blank).
25. Attended the King's leveée.
March 5. Attended drawing room, Queen's birthday, Lady Laurie did not go, very cold, but very full.
17. Attended Common Council and spoke against a resolution of the Committee of the whole Court, but no one supported me.
19. Attended Common Council and got seconded the resolution (recinding) the resolution which was carried last Tuesday, only one or two hands against recinding. This shews the necessity of persevering even if in a small minority, as very often good sense and justice ultimately prevail when least expected.
27. This day delivered in the following account of my receipts from the City during my year of office by the desire of a committee appointed to enquire into the expences of the office. From the chamber, locket etc total: £7904 1s 3d.
April 9. Having as magistrate of the Marlebone division refused to renew a licence to Mr Cleeve of Edgeware Road in consequence of his obtaining a licience for a tavern where it was much needed and afterwards converted it into a gin shope, this day he appealed to the Middlesex sessions, the appeal was dismissed by the court, 10 to 8. We also determined to grant a licience to a good house near any of the public houses which had converted their houses from public

houses to gin shops. One person not agreeing to the magistrate's directions was granted a licience to a good house which the new landlord named the Laurie Arms.

A grand dress party, Mansion House. Peel and his ministry resigned.

18. Lord Melbourne kissed hands as Minister and the old ministry delivered up their seals.

19. A fellow dressed like a gentleman could not guide his horse in the park, rode against me and bruised my knee very much and was laid up for a few days.

20. Easter Monday. Could not go to the Mansion House. Lady Laurie, Peter and Miss Laurence went.

Having made a speech *on the 18th March.* at the Common Council against periodical election, which having mad(e) a very great impression I published the same after it was corrected and greatly improved by Peter Laurie and this day sent nearly 100. I had answers from Lord Brougham and many others and the speech was considered good because it contained facts that could not be contradicted. Two replies were made from a Mr Norris and Franks, but no notice was taken of them and they deserved none. The speech was very favorably noticed in the 'Times' and 'Herald'. This was my first published work and I am much gratified with the effect produced.

26. Judges *at.* St Paul's and then dined Mansion House.

May 1. Attended Freemasons' and promoted an address to the King, etc.

11. A very grand dinner given to Peel at the Merchant Tailors' hall. I was a steward. Very hot, Peel great. 400 persons present, seats drawn by lot, Peel said the son of a cotton spinner had been sent for from Rome to make him prime minister and told us it was the Commons and not the Lords that we must look to for the preservation of our institutions.

12. Lord Mayor Winchester broke up the Court of Common Council in grand style.

15. A party went to Peel's to ask him to a dinner to be given him by Marlebone, which he, in my opinion, very properly declined. We returned to the coffee house and got up Mr Mackinnon's speech and Peel's and sent it to the newspapers. I took the affair in hand.

16. This day the members of the North British Life Office met and established a reversionary society making me chairman and Mr Warden deputy chairman.

22. Bishop's dinner, Mansion House.

23. A public breakfast, Victoria, steam boat, Wapping.

24. The Royal Highland school dinner, Lord Stanley in the chair, a splendid chairman. A grand day, 200 present.

26. This day I again moved and succeeding in opening the Court of Alderman to strangers, 13 to 5, and it has always been open since.

27. This day the Queen came to the Mansion House to see the examination of the national schools, several grandees present, but no arrangement, nothing like the Queen's visit to me the 13 June 1833.

28. Went to drawing room, King's birthday. Very crowded, took Peter, Lady Laurie did not go.
31. Sunday. Went to St Paul's at 3 o'clock and met Lord Denman and the other judges. Dined at home.
June 4. Did not go to Epsom.
8. Very hot.
9. For several days I went and got the holders of India Stock to sign affidavits to vote for Mr Warden; such a troublesome task I will not again undertake.
May 15. A deputation waited upon Peel to ask him to dine in the boro of Marlebone, which he declined and we put in the interview and speeches in papers. Before.
16. Bishops dined Mansion House. Before.
June 16. Dined Aldersgate, Dispensary Shepherd elected, *India House.*
July 3. Bridewell dinner.
4. Conservancy, Greenwich.
8. Viewed the extraordinary works of the Mint.
11. Heard O'Sullivan, Exeter Hall.
141. A special Court, Saddlers' Hall to receive my picture.
30. I felt so alarmed for the political consequences of the Municipal Bill, I wrote 15 letters and inclosed copies of my speeches on the subject to the 15 chief speakers of the House of Lords and had their answers, but when the Bill returned to the Commons, Peel gave way and I fear the consequences. We shall hve none but radical magistrats, none but radical members from the boroughs.
August 1. Accompanied the King to Greenwich with all the City state.
7. Was examined in the Lords respecting goals.
14. Saddlers' Court went to church.
15. Lady Laurie was taken dangerously ill at 1 o'clock in the morning. Peter went for Maclure, sat up all night. She remained very unwell for 7 days and was constantly, at least 3 days in the week, (seen) by McLure, Mr Hudson. The Receiver of Bethlem Hospital was detected of cheating and absconded, see Letts diary.
24. Lady Laurie and Miss Wilkie in an[120] open carriage hired from Jones went off to Ramsgate with coachman and footman and two coachhorses. The saddle horse and groom remained at home. Peter and I went by coach to the following places:
25. Stamford then to 26 Lincoln.
27. Hull to 28 York.
29. Harrogate to 30 Harrogate.
31. Leeds to Boroughbridge.
September 1. Appleby to September 2. Kendall.
3. Liverpool then to 4 Manchester.
5. Buxton to 6 Buxton.
7. Matlock to 8 Liechfield.

9. Leamington to 10 Cheltenham. 11 to 14. Cheltenham.
15. London, when I found Robert Peter Laurie dangerously ill.
17. Robert Peter Laurie died, leaving a young widow pregnant. His death was very unexpected, and in my opinion he had been greatly neglected or rather improperly treated by Mr Pettigrew, his surgeon. I had often requested him to have a additional advice but he had too much confidence in Mr Pettigrew. He was a generous warmhearted young man and I felt gretly distressed at his death. He made no will.
23. Robert Peter Laurie burried St George's burial ground, Hyde Park, Uxbridge Road. It was a heavy day to all his friends, cut of early in life, yet his constitution never was good. He was a very honorable, high minded, disinterested young man, was kind to all his relations.
October 2. Went to Ramsgate by coach to join Lady Laurie and Miss Wilkie at No. 7, Paragon. Remained at Ramsgate where we had carriages etc, the groom and saddle horses remaining in London, till the 15 when I came home by coach leaving the ladies to come home with my own horses which they did and returned on the 22. Horses etc all well. Peter did not go to Ramsgate but went with Colonel Clitherow and Anderton to Lincolnshire to see the Bethlem estates.
21. First stone of Corporation school laid by Lord Brougham and afterwards dined at the City of London Tavern.
28. John Laurie had his son, born 1 October 1835, baptised 28 September (sic) John Winborn Laurie and all dined, 32 party.
November 11. Settled Mrs Robert Laurie's affairs with John Laurie, and Peter Laurie, Jeffrey and self became trustees.
13 Mrs (Robert) Laurie having given birth to a boy on (blank he) was this 13 day of November, baptised Robert Peter Laurie and I became godfather.
30. The stewards of the Scots Hospital came and got me to take the chair, St Andrew's day. I reluctantly consented and after I was in the Tavern, the Duke of Gordon very unexpectedly arrived and took the chair, but behaved with the greatest kindness and gave my health after the King.
December 3. Court of Aldermen rejected Salomon because he refused to sign the declaration.
12. Peter and I went to Brighton and returned on the 15, a hard frost.
21. A wardmote and contest. Old members chosen.
27. Thomas Gray left London for New South Wales. Mr Mackinnon on behalf of the Conservatives offered to start me for the Borough of Marlebone. If I would give £500 they would pay all my expences. They had balloted for Lord Teignmouth, Sir F. Booth and myself after seeing Mr Hibble, the most active of the tradesmen, and examining the lists. I after many thanks for their preference, I[121] declined, seeing no prospect of success and not wishing to be beaten, being convinced that the Bōro is not yet ripe for a conservative, had the interview with Mr Mackinnon on the 4 January 1836.

1836.

January 8. Retired from the Commercial Railway.

16. Prevented Rotch being brot up for judgement.

February 22. Mr R. Price chosen treasurer, Bethlem. Attended very frequently the Committee of the whole Court, Common Council. See Letts diary.

26. Peter Laurie's excellent letter to Hume, 'Chronicle'.

March 2. Mrs Robert Laurie signed the trust deed appointing Sir Peter Laurie, Mr Jeffrey and Peter Laurie trustees.

16. Conservative meeting at Wigmore Street. They wrote to me to take a resolution, I attended, spoke but little as I promised to speak at the dinner.

Dinner room, Yorkshire Stingo, horridly hot. Made a good speech, but was interrupted by Dr Pope, see newspapers.

22. Met at Lloyds, floored Pope.

April 12. City Conservative dinner, 1038 in Covent Garden theatre, a brilliant sight, was a steward, cost £4.

26. Met the London and West Bank directors with Sir F. Booth and declined joining as we by the deed must hold stock for 12 months before we could take a seat in the direction, and wrote to Stewart to that effect, 28.

May 14. Scots' school anniversary dinner, Richmond, in the chair.

15. The eclipse of the sun.

19. Went to Lady Brownlow's party with Lady Laurie.

28. King's birthday, Peter and I went to drawing room.

June 3. Pettigrew having sent an infamous bill to Mrs (Robert) Laurie, it was refused payment, he brought an action and got a verdict minus £38, but as I advised to action, I paid the costs out of my own pocket, being determined she should sustain no loss in following my advice. The costs I paid were £(blank). The jury gave me a verdict against the summing up of the judge.

Began sitting to Lilley for a portrait for the North British Life Assurance Company.

9. Duchess of Kent, Mansion House.

11. Colonel Clitherow, Mr Price and myself went in a landaw and 4 horses, slept at Canterbury, where Mr Adams the accountant joined us. Viewed all our farms in Kent on the Saturday. Colonel Clitherow left us at Margate, where we slept, and came home in a Margate steam boat. We drove to Ramsgate and slept at Herne Bay and returned to London on Monday the 13.

14. My good and great friend Sir David Wilkie knighted.

July 1. Bridewell dinner, very hot.

23. Dined at Albion, a dinner given to Lord Elphinstone by the East India Company. Grand and hot.

29. Lady Laurie and Miss Wilkie left London with a calaiche, 2 horses *on hand, Rattler lame*, coachman and footman for Cheltenham.

August 5. Went at 10 o'clock with Mr Price, Mr Adams *and* Peter Laurie in an open landaw to Lincolnshire to receive rents and view our estates. Slept at Eaton,

then went next day to Wainfleet.
7. Went to Wainfleet church. Remained in Lincolnshire till Friday, went to Lincoln and got home to London on Saturday the 13.
20. Left London with Peter Laurie for Cheltenham, was very ill on the road, got better on Sunday.
22. Got to Bath, stopped all night at Bath. Went in the morning 23 with Sir David Wilkie and Peter Laurie, went to Bristol and met the British Association. Remained there till Friday the 26, for the particulars see papers. It was a humbug from first till last, but very entertaining.
27. We went to Taunton. 28. to Minehead. 29. to Linton. 30. to Ilfracombe.
31. Barnstable Cleveley.
September 1. to Exeter. 2. to Wills. 3. to Clifton. 4. to Chepstow. 5. to Cheltenham. Sir David left Cheltenham *10 September to attend Old Bailey sessions.*
19. Left Cheltenham for London, leaving Lady Laurie and Miss Wilkie at 18, Cambray. Lady Laurie having been taken ill with a sore throat on the 18, Dr Baron was called in and said she would be able to travel to Leamington on the 22d.
22. Heard from Miss Wilkie that Lady Laurie was *very* ill and could not go to Leamington. Heard every second day that Lady Laurie was improving in health sl(owly).
23. Remained attending the Old Bailey sessions and frequently hearing from Cheltenham that Lady Laurie was a little better. Attended the election of Mayor, Kelly chosen. The Sheriffs, Duke and Johnson, gave their inauguration dinner in the Egeptian Hall, a shably numerous company. Aldermen not properly seated and not pleased.
October 2. Hearing almost daily from Miss Wilkie that Lady Laurie was better and that she would start in a day or two, I did not go to Cheltenham. She had sent home the footman and had her maid sent down, but still Miss Wilkie said she was better. On the 2d October when we came home from Dodsworth's church I received a parcell by mail containing a letter from Miss Wilkie requesting me to come immediately to Cheltenham as Lady Laurie was dangerously ill. Peter and I took the chariot which had been left at home and had post horses, drove off at 3 o'clock for Cheltenham calling first at D. Wilkie's as he was to have dined in Park Square on that day. We lighted the lamps at Wycomb, it was a dreadful night for rain and storms and darkness. Got to Witney at half past twelve, took shelter for a short time. Got to North to breakfast and when we got to Cheltenham never can I forget the sight. Poor Lady Laurie could not lift her eyelids, said all human aid was now in vain, and kept continually hiccupping and was as helpless as a child.

Dr Baron came at 11 o'clock, I asked her complaint. He said she had a tumour in the pit of her stomach which caused constant heavings and sickness and nothing came up. The cries and tears of the poor sufferer was dreadful. They had called in Mr Murely and Dr Cannon. I firmly said there was no tumour, that she had always been subject to sickness and insisted that they would discontinue the treatment which had nearly destroyed her. They did so, and Mrs Turner, at whose house we were, had more skill than all the doctors. She had of her own accord got some jelly and we all sat up all night giving her some every half hour. At 4 in the morning she was easier and the hiccup ceased a little. At 7 in the morning a little better. Baron was astonished and after two more visits did not come again. Murley said he did not think it was a tumour but continued inflamation from the throat. Had the ignorant Doctor Baron continued to give her his drugs and had Peter and I not arrived when we did to stop her sickness she must have died in 24 hours. Mrs Turner said it was impossible she could last so long. Miss Wilkie(’s) constand care and skill and strong attachment was also greatly instrumental in preserving the life, for it was no longer the health which was in danger. The Reverend Dr Mr Brown also saw Lady Laurie and he agreed with me which was a great relief to Lady Laurie, for altho not a medical man he had great experience. In a week she got down to the drawing room.

12. On this day we attemped to move and got as far as North Leach. Lady Laurie no sleep. Next day to Witney and on the day following to Oxford. Peter and I coming short steps by the coach, Lady Laurie, Miss Wilkie and maid with my own horses. Peter and I came by coach from Oxford. The ladies got home on the 17 having slept at Henley and then at Salt Hill. This was the most trying fortnight I ever had and altho Mr Thomas Wilkie was so very ill yet his sister would not leave her friend. Her kindness I never can forget. Lady Laurie remained at home nursing till the 5 November 1836 when she took an airing for the first time.

November 9. Lord Mayor’s Day. Took Sir David and Miss Wilkie and Miss McGregor. The (day) went off as usual.

18. The Saddlers’ Company kept the centenary of Prince Edward being elected a member of their Company. I was requested to take the chair, which I did, and had the Lord Mayor etc.

23. Lady Laurie was able to go into the City and took her dividend.

26. Had the Lord Mayor and a party of gentlemen.

December 3. Dined with Sir W.Follett.

9. Brighton. Lady Laurie and I took post horses with chariot and reached Brighton in 8 hours. Servant on box got into the same house with the Wilkies in Devonshire Place. I had sent my 4 horses before me.

10. Hunted Matt a capital hunter. Mare too hot.

11. Very cold. Came to London 20 for St Thomas’s day.

30. The weather was most severe till the end of the year. No communication for some days between London and Brighton, the snow was so deep and frost so severe. Sir David Wilkie came and remained some time at Brighton, the King sitting to him. I had little or no hunting and was obliged to ride on the sands when the sea was out. Peter came and remained a week at Christmas.

1836.

January. Sir David and I remained until the 9th January when we returned to town. Left Lady Laurie and Miss Sparkes with coachman, chariot. Sent saddle horses to town. The weather most severe both at Brighton and indeed all over England. Peter very unwell, had Dr McLester. I was also very ill with the influenza, everybody ill.

February 8. Lady Laurie and Miss Sparkes returned from Brighton. Mr Slater coming from Mercer's Company fell, broke his leg, which was amputated and he died in consequence a few weeks afterwards. I made, in January, David Pollock a governor of Bethlem.

20. Smirke elected Bethlem 87, Mosely 17.

25. Ministers' dinner, Mansion House.

March 1. Not well, came from Old Bailey and took medicine.

24. Good Friday. Had the Wilkies to dinner, was hoarse from Christmas till this day.

27. Easter Monday. Dined City.

30. Spent the day Richmond. Peter joined me from sessions, Kingston.

April 1. Mary Ann Jack very ill.

16. Judges at St Paul's, dined Mansion House.

17. Dined with Reshid Bey, Turkish ambassador.

27. Attended Queen's birthday.

28. Got 500 for destitute Scots. 68 per 1000, 66 per 500. Got Mr Tulk to move for a return of all charges of felonry at all the offices and how disposed, which made Roe and others angry.

May 12. Got Chantry the Wellington statue, 15 to 14, 14 for Wyatt.

19. Heard that my brother Nichol died on the 11th, was buried 14, aged 70. Dined with the bishops. Alexander Reid whom I had put into Christ's Hospital 7 years ago, came out and saild for Van Demen's Land[122] where his father and mother had gone some years ago to seek their fortune.

27. Highland school dinner.

28. Sheriffs' sermon and dinner.

29. Drawing room, King's birthday.

30. Went up with an address to Duke of Kent and Princess Victoria.

June 3. Got a vote of censure upon Wilson for presenting a letter to Duke of Kent. Lady Laurie and Miss Wilkie went to Richmond and put up, Castle. I went Tilbury evening. Mrs Norton died. Drove to Hampton Court.

5. Lady Laurie and Miss Wilkie removed from Castle to Rose Cottage, Richmond, 4 guineas a week.

20. King William 4th died. The Lord Mayor and Aldermen went to Kensington, signed proclaimation, not in robes, took a hackey carriage.

21. Queen proclaimed.

23. Lady Laurie returned very unwell from Richmond, called in Maclure.

24. Carrol and Montifiore elected sheriffs.
26. McLure (sic) sent 20 bottles stuff to Richmond.
28. Scots' Hospital. Addresses, Peter wrote one.
July 1. Took David Wilkie to Richmond.
8. King William buried.
12. Went up, the City, with address to the Queen, St James's.
13. Went with an address to Queen Adelaide, Bushy Park.
18. Went up the river with the Lord Mayor's water party.
19. Lady Laurie and Miss Wilkie returned from Richmond, having been there 47 days. Queen's leveée attended.
24. Lady Laurie and Miss Jacks took lodgings at Hampstead.
25. City election, chosen Wood, Pattison, Crawford and Grote, Palmer only 6 below Groate.
26. Marlebone. Whalley and Hall, Tiegnmouth 395 below *Whalley.*
29. River party, 1st section.
August 4. Middlesex. Byng and Wood elected, Hume out.
7. Lady Laurie came from Hampstead 14 days, then D. Chambers called in to Lady Laurie.
22. Lady Laurie and Miss Wilkie went in open hired barouch with one hired horse and Rattler. Rattler fell ill at Rochester and returned. The ladies took post horses and went to Ramsgate.
26. Locum tenens for Lord Mayor for a week.
September 8. I went to Ramsgate, 7, Paragon, 6 guineas. Peter came down on the 5th.
13. John and his wife and Mrs Robert Laurie went to Scotland.
18. I returned from Ramsgate.
20. John, his wife and Mrs Robert Laurie went to Scotland.
22. Saw Mary Ann (Jack) for the last time who said truly that I should never see her again. She was in great pain.
24. Sunday. Peter went to Sloane Street, returned at 11 and said poor Mary Ann had died ½ past 3 in the morning. She never had strength and her life was a life of personal sufferings. She reached 50 years of age. Lady Laurie and Miss Wilkie returned from Kent, *Tunbridge Wells*.
26. Mr Wood, *a tory*, elected Aldersgate instead of Walton. Wood 43, Alcock 22, poll demanded. Close 95 to 64[123].
29. Cowan chosen Mayor. John and party returned from Scotland having been absent 15 days.
30. Mary Ann Jack burried in her father's tomb, Bunhill Fields. A respectable funeral but no shew or ostentation.
31. Attended Swallow Street church. Lady Laurie very ill and much distressed at her sister's death.

The Queen having accepted the invitation to dine on the 9th November and the aldermen having agreed to meet her on horseback which was carried with great difficulty, allowing those who chose to go in carriage, and the Common Council having appointed 6 of their members to ride with us, I was appointed master of the horse. Called upon Major General Vivian and asked him for horses, 27, 27 *manage*, he at once wrote to Colonel Jones, Woolwich and gave us our choice of 27 horses and I with Mr Anderton and Peter Laurie went and selected them.

October 9. Called upon the commander in chief and asked for a troop of Life Guards for the 9th November; agreed to.

11. Lady Laurie and Miss Wilkie went with post horses to Hastings.

16. Got extra tickets for the Aldermen who ride.

21. Opposed railing the streets from Guildhall to Temple Bar, for the foolish proposal 4, against 7. Also opposed giving the livery companies stands in the streets but recommended St Paul's churchyard.

24. At Home Office opposed the Queen returning in state. Mr Maule would not agree with me but afterwards the coachman came to me and we settled that the Queen was to return with a pair of horses only.

26. Ordered trappings for my troop of aldermen and horsemen at Pearce's and Paul's.

29. Went to Chapel Royal for the first time, wretched stuff, only a concert, no religion. I pity princes.

31. Attended riding school, Woolwich and selected the chargers.

November 2. Attended with a deputation on the City reform at Home Office, to me a very satisfactory interview. *Dined with the Lord Mayor elect at Wax Chandlers' hall, 40 dined.*

4. Lady Laurie and Miss Wilkie returned from Hastings. Lady Laurie not improved in health, had a bilious fever at Hastings.

6. Colonel Jones and Captain Teasdale brought up 28 horses to Mr Davis's riding school, Black Friers Road, and I had all the Aldermen and the 2 Lord Mayors mounted. We, to let them on, turned a pail up and they mounted upon the bottom of the pail. Ordered of Messers Pearce red horse clothes to go over the cavalry saddles, holsters etc with a leather surcough, the cloth edged (with) yellow silk beading which looked very rich. Called Horse Guards and said we wanted 800 troops, they had only 400 to spare with which number I should be content.

8. Dined with 2 Lord Mayors.

9. The artillery horses and one solder to each came to Temple Bar and went into the Temple and waited our arrival. I went in carriage with Miss Wilkie and Peter Laurie, a well kept line all the way. Got out at Child's and after a sumptous luncheon we went to mount our horses, but oh, what horse men, but for the soldiers holding the horses and the cavalry saddles with holsters they never could have remained on. We, upon my giving the word of command, rode to Temple Bar, the even numbers on the south side and when the Queen came, the procession was as follows:

Detatchment of Life Guards.
Duchess of Kent and attendants. 6 horses.
Duchess of Gloucester and ditto. 6 horses.
Duke and Duchess of Cambridge ditto. 6.
Duke of Sussex and attendants.
Her Majesty's carriages:
1st carriage , 6 grays , sword of state
2d. ditto , 6 bays , Equerry in waiting
3d. ditto , 6 bays , Treasurer
4. ditto , 6 bays , Lord in waiting
5. ditto , 6 bays , Maid of honor
6. ditto , 6 blacks, Lady bedchamber
7. yeomen of the guard.
12 footmen 4 and 4.
Police officers on horseback.
The state carriage of the sheriffs.
The state coach of the late Lord Mayor.
The Lord Mayor's state coach.
City Marshalls on horseback.
Members of the Common Council on horseback:
James Anderton esq. Richard Dixon esq.
Joshua J. Bedford esq. William Collingwood esq.
William Hunter esq. W.A.Peacock.
The Sheriffs in their scarlet gowns and chains, each attended by a sergeant and groom:
Moses Montifiore. George Carroll.
Aldermen in their scarlet gowns and chains, attended by groom and beadle:
John Humphrey. James White.
Thomas Wood. James Harmer.
W.J. Copeland. H. Winchester.
C. Farebrother. Sir P. Laurie.
Sir John Key. W. Thompson.
M.P. Lucas. W. Venables.
Sir W. Heygate. M. Wood.
Sir C. Hunter.
The Right Honorable Thomas Kelly, late Lord Mayor.
Common Cryer on horseback: Samuel Beddome.
The Sword bearer on horseback: C.W. Hick.
The Lord Mayor on horseback, crimson robe and collar of SS, bearing the City sword of state.
The state coach, 8 cream coloured horses.
The Queen.
Mistress of the Robes.

Master of the horse.
Escort of Life Guards.

At St Paul's the boys of Christ's Hospital assembled and the senior scholar delivered an address when the Queen arrived, council chamber, the Recorder addressed Her Majesty in an address. Her Majesty returned an anser and created the Lord Mayor a baronet, and knighted the two Sheriffs.

The 6 senior Aldermen preceeded Her Majesty from the Council Chamber to the dinner table. The same form was observed upon Her Majesty's retiring. Nothing could have been better arranged, not a single accident occurred. It rained during our procession from Temple Bar, but as we had the large coronation hat and garters to slip over our silk stockings, we were not in the least inconvenienced by the slight rain. The streets were of course crowded. There were (blank) guests and members of the Corporation.

The whole expence was £8,172 4s 11d. An account of the whole was printed and sent to each member of the Corporation.

16. The Lord Mayor and sheriffs gave their usual dinner, very hot and crammed. I took Mrs Barnes. Lord Ramsay could not attend, sent his ticket back and I gave it to B. Boyd.

24. *Post article and my letter about appointing magistrates for Marlebone.*

28. At Court of Aldermen Hunter proposed and I seconded that in future the dinner to the judges should not be on a Sunday. I took some pains in this.

31. Miss Jack took out probate on 1st December, under £5000.

December 3. The Lord Chancellor having promised to appoint 15 magistrates in Marlebone of liberal opinion, I waited upon Lord Abinger who said he would write to Lord Wharncliffe.

5. Waited on Lord Wharncliffe who promised to look after the Lord Chancellor, left him all the papers.

21. Held wardmote, and afterwards the Common Council dined in Park Square.

22. Mr Elliott, Mr Pepys and Peter Laurie *and I* waited upon the Lord Chancellor who asked if we would act with the new magistrates he intended to appoint. We said we would do our duty but that they were not wanted, nothing had been regulated. He admitted this, only would magistrates of liberal opinions? We told him there were 10 tories and 10 whigs and 3 I did not know their opinions. I left him *the paper with the names.*

25. Chrismas day I kept as usual but no Mary Ann, the first death in our family for several years.

1838.

January 10. The Royal Exchange burnt. A dreadful night, the snow so thick the streets impassable.

11. Summoned to Mansion House to take steps respecting the Exchange's iron chests and papers in Mayor's court. Very cold.

23. Mrs John Laurie delivered of a boy, baptized Peter George.
February 1. County day, Middlesex. The county asylum for lunatic at Hanwell requiring investigation, I moved to recind the former law which made those who had attended the fewest times to retire, which was a great abuse as the Superintendent always got his friends to attend and they supported him in all lobbing. Carried that the 3d of the committee should retiere by seniority which caused the Superintendent Ellis to resign and a thorough reform in the asylum.
26. Court of Aldermen agreed to oppose the new police. A most severe winter, pipes frozen for months and water came by tapping the pipe letting in the air.
March 3. Teigmouth 4166, Ewart 3762, Thompson 186 for Marlebone. Examined by House of Commons.
April 4. Having got Mr Fraser to put legs to my portrait painted by Phillips for which I gave him £40, I this day presented it to Bridewell and Bethlem committee with a letter and received a complimentary answer and the portrait hung up in the hall on 9th April.
18. Very cold and snow.
May 18. To avoid 3 public dinners Peter and I went to Brighton and Hastings and returned 21th.
June 28. The coronation; having fully given all account of it in Letts dairy, I do not repeat it here. It was the same as the coronation of William the 4th.
30. Lady Laurie and Miss Wilkie went to Tunbridge Wells.
July 3. The City having agreed to give the foreign ambassadors a dinner, I attended committee, got one half of the invitations for conservatives.
5. Attended review Woolwich South etc etc.
13. The grand entertainment to the ambassadors.
14. Sir D. Wilkie and I went to Tunbridge and returned 16.
21. Sir David and Peter and I went to Windsor by rail road and returned by Southampton rail road 23d.
26. It having been agreed to erect additional buildings at[124] Bethlem we agreed to have a splendid day in laying the lst stone and it was so splendid and so satisfactory that Peter Laurie was requested to draw up a narrative of the proceedings which he did and has been published *and sent* to the governors. 620 dined in the tent.
30. Lady Laurie and Miss Wilkie returned from Tunbridge.
August 1. Attended meeting London Tavern to promote a subscription for a monument to Nelson. Wellington in the chair. I *spoke and* was much applauded.
9. Lady Laurie and Miss Wilkie went to Brighton. Price, Adams, Peter Laurie and I went to view our estates in Oxfordshire, returned 11th.
18. Peter and I went to Brighton, all 4 horses there, returned 28 September. Lady Laurie and Miss Wilkie going to Tunbridge Wells 29.
October 25. Lady Laurie and Miss Hopkins returned from Tunbridge Wells.
November 2. Peter Laurie in his pamphlet on grand juries, a clever work, stated that a clerk should attend to grand juries. This was some years ago and the

idea has been approved by all who understand the subject. I wrote to Lord Denman, he attended this day and proposed it to the judges, 10 of them all that attended agreed *with him, in all 11,* and they unanimously appointed the clerk of the Aragin's Mr Clerk, to the office and this was indeed a victory.
4. In the 'Despatch' sunday paper there was a libel upon me in consequence of my observations in a case at Guildhall. Peter consulted Sir W. Follett and they determined to file a criminal information. Mr Harmer agreed to make any apology I required, Peter wrote the apology, a very humble one and one condition was it was to be in a large type. All this they published on the 11th.
December 14. Completed the purchase of the ground facing Bethlem hospital for £ (blank) thus preventing the Roman Catholics taking the ground and building a cathedral. I had a very difficult task but I completed it.
19. Had poor old Rattler, a horse I had for 14 years, shot. He was gay to the last but no strength.
21. At my wardmote 2 conservatives returned instead of radicals, now a conservative ward.

1839.
January 9. Mr Webster and the Messers Boyds had very often mentioned that they wished to establish a new joint stock bank in London closely united with the Scots banks. I had as often declined, but upon proposing to add Mr Peter Laurie for his sake to give him employment I consented and our first meeting was on Wednesday the 9th January 1839, when we had a board of excellent directors, approved of prospectus.
17. Peter carried a motion at Middlesex county court to have a clerk to attend grand jury.
28. Took house in Moorgate Street for bank at £435 per annum.
February 4. Opened our bank and had nearly all our shares sold from our good advertisments and good names and good manager, Mr Scrimgeour from Bank of England, gave him £1000 a year.
25. £6000 placed in Bank of England in trustee's name to pay to Chantrey as per deed. Trustees Peter Laurie, Masterman, Barclay and Jones and paid over £(blank) to Chantrey with the metal which Sir Francis received from the government, and I have no doubt it will be a statue worthy of the Duke of Wellington.
March 11. Attended with a deputation Lord J. Russell against the introduction of the metropolitan police into the City. A very unsatisfactory reply from cunning John Russell.
17. Called upon Gouldbaum with the Aldersgate petition for him to present and begged of him to see Peel and adwise him not to take part against the City for it was a lever by which we would greatly damage if not remove the ministry.
21. The Corporation went to Buckingham Palace with the address begging Her Majesty not to interfere with the privileges of the City, the largest number that

ever went upon any occasion. A very unsatisfactory rambling reply from the Home Secretary Lord J. Russell. We made two radicals kiss the Queen's hand, Galloway and Stacy, pretending that they were the mover and seconder of the address, making the radicals work our work and fight our battles, for this measure was by the Conservatives more considered a political than a civic matter.

25. Bank. Opened branch in Argyll Place.

April 2. Settled the deed at the bank.

15. Attended Mansion House when Mr Clarkson had his bust presented to him. Thomas Wood proposed, I the seconder. A very fine old man[125] ill used by Wilerbeforce's life.

19. My chesnut mare fell *twice* having a fit of palsy. The groom not hurt. She recoverd thro Field's treatment but fell again in November and was sold a Tattersalls for 23 guineas. When once a horse like a man has a fit, sure to have a second. Beat the radicals in Common Council, 17 majority against reducing the numbers of Common Councilmen.

May 6. An evening party.

7. Ministers. The wretched Whig Ministers having only a majority of 5 resigned. Peel sent for.

10. The Queen refused to give up her chamberwomen. Sir R. Peel declined forming a ministry. Melbourne sent for and take the reins of government again. The explanation of this disgraceful juggle in House of Commons, 13 May.

16. City conservative. Sir M. Wood who represents the Whig ministry in the Corporation called 15 of his party out of the Common Council. Jones went by mistake into the room where they were assembled and they told him they ment to address the Queen to thank her for taking back Melborne and his crew. Jones wrote to me, went on Saturday the 18th, and having beaten the radicals on the 3 July 1838 upon the attempt to give a dinner to the ambassadors and the ministers, I knew by proper management we might beat them again.

Having moved Alderman Brown to the chair, I from the pocket book called over the names and founds we had a majority. Gaddesden voluntarily became secretary, Mr King was requested to print circulars to call us together when the requisition was given to the Lord Mayor. I called daily and found on the Lord Mayor got the requisition for, and ordered a Common Council on the Thursday, 30. Our conservative meeting was held on Monday 27, when we resolved to meet the mottion to go to the Queen with the previous question and Anderton to move and I to second. The radicals now knew their weakness and would have withdrawn it but we sent another circular requiring members not to leave the Common Council until the vote.

We met at (?), lead 6 or 7 on the 30th and were determined to force them on, and at 12 Ashust *and Norris* moved and seconded the address, Anderton and I the previous question. Our side; Brown, Gaddesden, *and Alderman* Heygate, against; Stevens, Thomas Wood, Taylor, Bayliss, Wire. 121 for the previous question, 75 against, a majority of 46. The government sent every half hour to know the result and nothing during their weak administration ever gave them such a heavy blow, and I must candidly say but for Alderman Brown, Jones and myself it would not have been carried.

31. Dowager Queen. Called upon the Lord Mayor with a requisition to vote an address of congratulation upon her coming back to England. I gave the address to the reporter at the Mansion House, it appeared 1 June, Saturday. Upon the evening of Saturday I received a letter from Lord Howe directed to 'my dear Sir Peter' and declining to name the address intended for publication and a private note to myself to prevent the matter going forward. I wrote and got some alterations in the public letter which was returned and Peter Laurie wrote copies for all the morning papers and they appeared on Monday the 3 June. Another victory for the Conservatives.

June 6. Lady Laurie and Miss Jack went to Brighton.

22. Committee met and voted for models, Nelson Monument. The Duke of Wellington proposed me as a scruitinere, I was much flatered by it. Railton 17, Lough 14, Bailey 14, Campbell 13, Woodegate 9, Hopper 2 and others 2.

July 5. Lady Laurie and Miss Jack and Miss Nicol returned from Brighton.

17. Bridewell feast well attended.

24. Lord Mayor's party up the river. I declined to go to Henley or Clifton Springs, but went with Lady Laurie, Miss Wilkie by railroad to Windsor to tea.

25. Saw the castle, drove to Virginia Water, dined and went to *a* ball at the town hall.

26. Returned by water after visiting Mr Hascourt, dined on board.

August 1. Went to Wainfleet with Price, Peter Adams. Remained in Lincolnshire till the 7. Returned on the 8 by railroad from Melton Mowbray, see dairy.

13. Lady Laurie and Miss Wilkie went in chariot to Leamington.

17. I went to Leamington. Peter went by the same railroad to Ireland.

27. I returned to London.

September 4. Peter returned from Leamington.

14. I went to Isle of Wight to meet Lady Laurie and Miss Wilkie who had travelled across the country from Leamington to Ryde.

21. Left the Isle of Wight, remained 2 days Portsea, a shocking place, returned to town 23 and the ladies went to Brighton, see dairy.

28. This day Mr Cator the Lord Mayor's chaplain preached a sermon before the election and reflected upon the characters of Wesley and Whitfield. Ordered to be printed by the Court of Aldermen before he received his vote of thanks.

October 3. Went to Brighton. Lady Laurie and Miss Wilkie returned 17 October.

November 9. Lady Laurie went with me to the Lord Mayor's Day.

25. This day sent Dr Crombie's letter of resignation as chaplain and secretary to the 'Society for Propagation Christain Knowledge' and sent in my own resignation for the same reasons that the parent board had missapplied the funds by

giving Mr Thomson at Mr Nickerson's request a piece of plate worth (£)150. I was treasurer 25 years but my constant labour as an alderman made me very anxious to give up the office and I availed myself of the opportunity.
30. I opposed a vote of thanks to Mr Cator for his sermon because he attacked Wesley and Whitfield and he had no thanks for his sermon.
December 9. Sat to Sir David Wilkie for portrait. Peter asked by Bonham to stand for Falmouth which I declined.
11. A very long letter in this day's 'Times' addressed to me from Mr Cator who vindicates his sermon and condems my remarks in Common Council and this 12 December I got Peter Laurie to assist and my reply appeared in the 'Times' justifying my opposition to his vote of thanks. From no exertions have I ever got such unqualified praise as from this letter except from the sect the Puzzites[126]. Later correspondence copied into 'Standard' and 'Herald', and the Wesleyans in consequence sent and asked me to take the chair at the anniversary of their missionary meeting, which will be noticed, 4 May 1840.

1840.
January 4. John's christning of Julius Dyson and a grand dinner.
10. This day the foolish penny post plan began. 2000 put in danger from Mr Dappa's death and the neglect of my agent Mr Sewell to insure his life. When I threatned an action against Sewell, who gave me a bond to pay the same in 4 years by equal instalments.
22. The sheriffs of London, Evans and Wheelton having served a process upon the printer of the House of Commons, Hansard, the House imprisoned them in one of their rooms belonging to the House[127]. We, Court of Aldermen and Common Council met and voted them thanks for their firmness etc and the important question of privileges lasted till a Bill was brought in in May. The sheriffs remained in confinement till their health gave way and were allowed to go out till called for, Wheelton by certificate from his M.D. that he was subject to applexy and by motion of Graham for Evans.

Purchased a 'Grant's Journal' which had a curious critic upon me, Grant a perfect stranger to me, whon the whole favorable.
February 7. A Common Hall petition to release the sheriffs.
10. Queen Victoria married to Prince Albert.
20. County meeting, Peter moved address to Queen and Prince on their marriage.
21. A meeting to petition the House of Commons *to release the sheriffs* by the Middlesex magistrates and others. The radicals with O'Connell, Hume, Wakely took possession of the Hall at the Freemasons, such a row as I never beheld. We tumbled Hume out of the chair, read the Riot Act and broke up the meeting, called another meeting for the 28, at the same place, took and kept possession of the Hall. Peter *Laurie* moved and Gibbons seconded resolution

with under sheriff France in the chair. A glorious victory over the radicals, the speeches excellent and all appeared on the 29 February.
March 3. Presented the City address at Buckingham House by the City upon the Queen's marriage.
6. Attended leveée with address's from county.
17. At Court of Aldermen got report giving up the justice room in the borough agreed to.
May 4. Took the chair at the Wesleyan annversary meeting at the Exeter hall. My speech greatly applauded and frequently quoted.
6. Lady Laurie taken ill, sent for Wade who came 3 times a day.
27. Lady Laurie and Miss Jack went to Tunbridge Wells.
June 10. The Queen shot at with powder by E. Oxford.
20. Lady Laurie and Miss Jack went to Ramsgate.
22. The City presented an address for the Queen's escape.
July 4. Opened Blackwall railway.
6. Courvoisier the Swite executed for murder (of) Lord William Russell.
8. The first annual meeting of the Union Bank, all unanimous and pleased at our unexampled prosperity. I was chosen governor for a second year and Spottiswood deputy governor.
23. Lady Laurie and Miss Jack came home from Ramsgate.
August 1. All the *Union* Bank directors dined with Barnes.
8. A holliday at St Albans, 3 days with Lady Laurie and Peter. Dull.
16. Sir David Wilkie sailed with Mr Woodburn in the 'Bataver' for Rotterdam at 7 o'clock.
20. Lady Laurie and Miss Wilkie went to Brighton.
28. Prince Albert having agreed to receive the freedom of the City and dine with the Lord Mayor, he came to Guildhall and received the freedom in the Hall and went to the Mansion House, but the Queen would not allow him to dine and he went away and all dined without him.
29. Alexander Laurie came from Scotland to go into the Bluecoat school.
September 3. Went to Brighton to join Lady Laurie, house New Steene and took 4 horses, 2 carriage and 2 saddle.
28. Sent saddle horses home and Peter and I returned to London.
29. *Alderman* Harmer[128] being in rotation for Lord Mayor, but being chief proprietor of the 'Weekly Despatch' a blackguard newspaper, the livery were determined to prevent his being elected and we took up Johnson and Pirie. The return was Harmer and Pirie. A poll was demanded for Johnson.
October 6. Close of the poll. Pirie 2741, Johnson 2713, Harmer 2294, majority 419. A great religious and Conservative triumph.
8. Court of Aldermen, 11 for Johnson and 3 for Pirie. I promisd to do the Mansion House duty every alternate Wednesday during Johnson's year to enable him to go to Romford, otherwise he would not have accepted the office being 75

years of age, but I was anxious to secure the services of a good, firm Conservative. I was sorry to take so active a part against a good temper'd man like Harmer but men must be guided by principle.

10. Hugh Richards who married my neice and who was most kind to me when I came to London died this day after a very long illness, aged 68. A very clever man and had he been a sober and a regular man would have easily have been a distinguished one. He has left my neice in small but independent circumstances.

16. Richards buried Highgate cemetry.

23. Lady Laurie and Miss Wilkie returned from Brighton.

November 4. This day my brother Robert Laurie of Rose Hill near Haddington died aged 81. It was always a most gratifying circumstance in my life that I could assist my relations as well as friends. I had bound down, as my brother expressed himself, to do nothing and he lived for the last 25 years on my bounty and I am sure he would have done the same for me had our cases been reversed.

9. Attended Guildhall dinner, as usual Lady Laurie did not go.

20. Princes(s) Royal born.

December 4. Sergeant Adams having charged the Bethlem court of improper treatment, the government send Dr Southey and Mako who reported in our favor after a long investigation.

5. Sinking the 'Dryad'. Began an investigation at the Mansion House of the two Wallaces for sinking the ship 'Dryad'. The enquiry in this case occupied nearly a month, the mercantile world were greatly interested in it. Peter was added to the counsel and they were tried at Old Bailey March sessions 1841 and found guilty. I had much praise of my firmness in refusing bail and protecting the shipping interest. The bill came to nearly £6000. A very hard frost for 18 days to 29 December.

1841.

January 16. A thaw after 34 days of hard frost and very cold.

17. A correspondance with Lord Normanby respecting Bethlem, published in the 'Times'.

28. Got Powers to take Lady Laurie and Miss Jacks, dined out.

29. Having, in vertue of my office as president of Bethlem, appointed Sir Robert Peel a governor of the royal hospitals, Bridewell and Bethlem, he declined the honor by saying he (had) not time and never took any office the duties of which he could not fulfill.

February 3. Went with Corporation address to the Queen at Buckingham House upon the birth of her first daughter.

11. Exposed the billing of the West Middlesex at the Mansion House which is one of the most extensive swindling concern ever know. Two obscure bad men put in names of persons well known such as Drummond etc only changing the Christian name, thereby getting between 2 and 300,000 from the public under

the pretence of insuring their lives or granting annuities and the people were completely robbed of that extraordinary amount.
20. Lord Mayor's dinner to the Ministers.
25. The Corporation voted thanks to Stoppard, Walker, Smith and Napier.
March 4. Wallaces found guilty of sinking a ship.
29. Visited Hertford and found Alexander Laurie doing no good at the Bluecoat school.
April 2. My picture by Wilkie sent to the exhibition Royal Academy.
12. Easter Monday. Had Lady Wilcock, got Sir H. top table.
20. Carried motion discontinuing the town hall, as it was intended as a job for Sir John Key.
May 13. In consequence of Peter Laurie and my own exertions we got a committee of the House of Commons to examine into joint stock companies. Peter and I were examined. Mr Shiel chairman, Granville Somerset took the lead, very clever.
19. A debate on the Corn Laws, Common Council. Against them 81, for continuing 65, majority 16, a radical victory.
21. Went to drawing room.
June 1. Lady Laurie, Miss Wilkie took possession of Brockhill Hall, Edgeware Road, for a month or two.
8. Wilkie's death. This day had a letter from Woodburn stateing that Sir D. Wilkie died 1 June of Gibraltar *in the steam boat from Malta* and had a watery grave. I never felt more for the loss of a friend, he was expected every day at home. Sent groom to bring up Lady Laurie and Peter to communicate or break the intelligence to Miss Wilkie at Kensington where she went to welcome him home.
11. Lady Laurie went to Kensington to remain with Miss Wilkie.
24. Magnay and Rogers elected sheriffs.
28. City election[129]. Candidates: Masterman, Lyall, Pirie, Wood, Crawford, Pattison, Attwood, Lord John Russell. I should have been one but was treacherously used by Alderman Thompson and the Conservative committee. After the 2d poll numbers: Masterman 6339, Wood 6315, Lyall 6290, Russell 6212, Attwood 6203, Pattison 6070, Crawford 6065, Pirie 6017. I voted for Lyall, Pirie and M. Wood.
July 1. Marlebone election. Voted for Cabbell and Hamilton. Hall 4461, Napier 4587, Hamilton 3383, Cabbell 3410.
7. Middlesex election. Byng and Wood, election without opposition. Dined with Wood, Cavendish Square.
12. Attended the annual meeting of the Union Bank, declared 5 per cent. All went off well, only a little grumbling at our taking the Charing Cross branch. I was reelected governor.
13. Peter inserted a paragraph calling a meeting to promote a subscription for a Wilkie statue.

25. Sent Alexander Laurie back to Scotland as he had not capacity to learn English being so deaf.
29. Held a meeting, the first, of the *London* Reversionary Society which gave great satisfaction to the shareholders.
August 11. Lady Laurie and Miss Wilkie went to Broadstairs.
13. Price, Adams, Peter and Frank Price went in an open carriage to view the Bethlem estates. Slept first night at Canterbury, 2d day viewed Walmer, slept Ramsgate, 3 day Ramsgate, 4 day Canterbury, 5 day home.
21. Started at the Paddington station with Price, Peter and self booked at Bolt in Tun for Cheltenham, dined at 10, slept 2d day, Sunday, at Cheltenham, 3d day Star, Oxford, 4 day *home.*
26. Wilkie's memorial committee met 7, Park Square, the general meeting took place 28, Peel in the chair. A splendid meeting. Present the Duke Sutherland, Lord James Russell, Lord Mahon etc, all will no doubt be in Cunningham's life of Wilkie. I and Peter were appointed treasurers, Allan and P. Cunningham secretaries. It was gratifying but painful, to lose so able, so good a friend was no ordinary loss.
September 2. Went to Lady Laurie and Miss Wilkie at Dover. Left Dover 6 September.
10. Lady Laurie and Miss Wilkie returned. Attended the funeral of William Brunton, a very quiet, good man, at Regent's church.
19. Committee of London Estates, took a view and dined.
29. Pirie elected Lord Mayor. Dined Mansion House.
30. Sheriff's dinner, Magnay and Rogers, at Albion and as usual.
October 1. A snug hole and corner meeting, advertised a meeting at the Mansion House *for 'Times' testimonial* got up by Wilson Alderman and Hughes. My name was not on the committee but Peter and I went, he wrote the resolution and I spoke and we did as like floored all opponents.
2. Lady Laurie went by coach to Ramsgate.
9. A dinner given by the Lord Mayor, Johnson, to the new ministry, Peel Prime (Minister).
12. Viewed Bethlem property, dined at Freemasons'. *Very wet.*
22. Set off for Brandsburton, Yorkshire with Kelly and Firth. Met Sir M. Wood at Dus Hotel, Birmingham where we slept. 2d day at Brandsburton where we remained till 27, viewing the property, hearing charges against the agent etc etc. Went to Scarborough, slept *Castle* Howard, then slept at York, a bad inn. 29 slept at Derby. Got home on Saturday 30. Dined Euston Square Hotel, see dairy.
November 2. Lord Mayor elect, Pirie, dinner Albion attended.
9. Prince of Wales born at 11 o'clock great rejoicing. Dinner at Guildhall, all the ministers there and Pirie congratulated upon his expected baronetcy. Pirie is the most lucky man I ever knew. I never had any luck, all my good fortune has been by exertion.

December 16. Mr Sergeant Arabin died. Canvassed for Peter Laurie to be common pleader in the event of Mr Bullock being made sheriff's judge and *met* with a most friendly reception, although canvassing was against a bye—law of the Corporation, and continued to canvass daily. Peter would have been disqualified as a candidate if he had canvassed.

1842.

January. Continued canvassing until I had seen every member of the Corporation.

17. This day Prince Albert laid the foundation stone of the new Royal Exchange and dined with the Ministers at the Mansion House.

27. Went up with an address to the King of Prussia at Buckingham House.

29. Slipped upon the steps which were like ice, hurt myself. The medical man I employed, Mr. Chisholm, put my accident in an extravagant paragraph and all my friends came alarmed. I was obliged to go to the justice room to prove I was not so ill.

February 17. Common Council recinded the bye-law against canvassing and Peter took the field, canvassed himself.

24. Common Council agreed to have but one judge for sheriff's court.

28. Bullock elected judge of the sheriff's court.

March 3. Mr Laurie's friends, 28, met all zeal carried resolutions.

5. Woodthorpe Town Clerk died.

12. Corporation addressed the Queen upon birth of Prince of Wales at Buckingham House.*24*. This was one of the most gratifying days in my life. The 3 candidates, Riddell Sir Walter, John Locke and Peter Laurie presented their petitions at the bar to be elected common pleader. The show of hand was taken according to the bye-law, where the two who had the biggest shew went to the poll[130], and Laurie and Locke had the shew of hands. Riddell retiering. When at the close of the poll Laurie had 112 votes, Lock 75, majority 37, 18 aldermen promised and 16 voted, whereupon Mr Laurie was declared common pleader and was introduced to his seat at the table. This was indeed a victory, when it is considered that Locke had been a candidate 8 years ago and Riddell was taken up by the Conservative Club. It proved that I was repected by the Corporation, that they appreciated the talents of my nephew and had not forgotten my public services and it is an event which I will ever think of with pleasure and gratitude.

April 12. Peter Laurie sworn inn as common pleader.

25. Agreed that the president was elected for life and not annually as had been done in Glyn's time.

29. Mr Dandbury brought Mr Pearson who had seen a man present a pistol at the Queen in St James's park but he stuttered so much that his brother who was with him had to repeat the statement he had made to him when he was not excited or afraid. I wrote a note and sent them to Buckingham Palace to the Honourable Mr Murray the Comptroller, and an alteration in the Queen's airings was made

by an equery riding at each door of her carriage which prevented her from being shot on the 30 when the same man, Francis, fired at the Queen, missed fire and was taken and examined by Privy Council.
30. The sale of Wilkie pictures and drawings finished and the (sale) fetched double what was expected.

Court of *Aldermen*. Met and agreed to address the Queen upon her escape. The Common Council objected to a separate address. I suggest in Common Council if they agreed with ours there would be but one and that would be from the Corporation.
June 15. Went up with an address *from the Corporation* to the Queen, Buckingham House.
17. Francis tried and found guilty of high treason.
24. Hooper Alderman and Mr Pilcher elected sheriffs.
27. *Lady Laurie and Miss Wilkie went to Scotland.*
29. Dined with Her Majesty's ministers at Goldsmith's *Hall.*
July 2. Wilkie statue committee, Peel in the chair, Joseph elected to make the statue. Vote Joseph 26, Campbell 13, Bailey 5, Watson 3.
16. Went by railroad to Brighton, came home on 18th. Brighton very hot and I was not well.
21. Declined going with the Lord Mayor to Rochester.
August 11. Went with Price, Peter Adams and Moore to visit Bethlem estates in Lincolnshire, where we remained there till the 18 and got home by train Saturday the 20.

On my return found a letter that my sister Agnes, the last remaining of our family, died on the 15 August.
25.[131] Peter and I went by mail to Dover. Slept at the York. Embarked for Ostend 26 and reached Antwerp ½ past 9.
27 and 28. Antwerp and Rotterdam. **29 and 30.** Rotterdam and Hague.
September 1 and 2. Saardam, Utrecht and Rotterdam. **3.** Rotterdam. **4 and 5.** Rotterdam and Antwerp. **6 and 7.** Brussells and Courtrai. **8 and 9.** Lille and Dunkirk. **10 and 11.** Calais. **12.** Reached Dover.
12 and 13. Dover and London. Lady Laurie and Miss Wilkie *returned 13 from Scotland.*

In Letts' diary I have copied my scrapes of notes and the occurrenes of each day. I think Holland the most extraordenary country I ever saw. The embankment, the cleanness of the houses, slovenlyness of the women, the fine pictures, the solemnity of the sabbath, the crudity of the people, not forgetting the horrid stench and dung hills in their streets and canals. I am glad I have seen Holland. The weather rather too hot.
29. Wood and Humphrey returned by the livery, Court of Aldermen returned Humphrey.
October 6.. Left London by train, slept Derby, then to Hull, Beverley, Brandsburton where we viewed the estates. Heygate, Magnay, Firth and son

went. Heygate returned Monday, we returned by Malton, York, Harrogate, Derby and got back to London Tuesday 18th, all detailed in Letts' diary.
19. Agness and Barbra, John's sisters came on a visit to him and remained a fortnight.
November 9. Lord Mayor's Day, Humphrey mayor. I took (?), had Mrs Dickens and Mrs Glennie.
11. A very extraordinary case came before me and it is thus mentioned in the 'Illustrated News'.

'The next and perhaps the most important bold step taken by Sir Peter was the enquiry he made into the proceedings taken by the Caoutchouc Company to protect their patent. The Company had prepared bills in Chancery against 51[132] tradesmen, in about 30 cases the solicitor had quietly compromised on paying him costs, thus preventing the matter from coming to a public hearing etc etc. The retail dealers and others concerned watched for an opportunity of finding Sir Peter on the bench to asssist them, but no such opportunity was likely to occur. They asked Sir John Pirie, then Lord Mayor, to allow Sir Peter Laurie to sit for him one day which he kindly granted and the hearing was obtained 4 November 1842. It was a scene of extraordinary excitment, the proceeding was adjourned to the Guildhall justice room and the result was that to the great joy of the retailers who had compromised and paid an amount of above £300, Mr Leaf the chief proprietor paid back all the money and his representative even consented to take the bills of the file of Chantry at his expence. One of the sufferers emphatically thanked God that the City of London had such a magistrate as Sir Peter Laurie and the whole body cheered the sentiment with great enthusiasm. Sir Peter said nothing had given him greater satisfaction in the course of his magisterial duty than this happy conclusion.'

The same paper says:

'Well known[133] he is, but with all that he has done there has generally been combined so much shrewdness and clear common sense, so much of independence of thought, ability to see the spirit of the law apart from its letter and determination to pursue the first even against the strict interpretation of the latter that he has not only effected an immense amount of public good but at the same time a creditable reputation. Bubble companies and swindling associations, the imposture of all kinds which this great city abounds have in Sir Peter Laurie a most determined and active enemy. On the whole he has the fullest right to the first place in our series of the City magistrates.'

This with many other remarks and cases quoted was published with a portrait, 21 January 1843[134].
26. The active part I took in exposing bubble companies caused a letter signed

R. Nicholson to appear in the 'Times' calling upon me to give an account of my conduct as an active director in the Equitable Loans bank, and on Monday a most triumphant reply was in the 'Times' written by Peter Laurie from documents I had very fortunately kept and no further enquiries were made. This shews the advantage of keeping records and any newspaper reports.

December 15. My favourite horse Tommy broke his knees *to the bone* but altho I was on he jumped instantly up. Never ride him again.

24. Bought a gray horse from Dye, well bred. Fine warm weather, not like winter.

1843.

January 1. This day heard with great pain Penfold preach upon the Puseyite forms recommended by the bishop of London and heard him thank God he had partly anticipated these form, while he had often told me he abhored them. I then resolved never to go there again while that mummery was continued and gave up my pew.

9. Appealed against to amount of rent rated by collector for income tax and had my appeal allowed.

15. A hard frost. Saw the Life Guards, Blues, dismount and lead their horses across Oxford Street as they could not stand upon wood pavement. This led me to take up the question of wood pavement which I opposed with all the zeal in my power.

25. Abused wood pavement at justice room Guildhall and published my collected number of falls of horses obtained from policemen.

27. Abusive article against me in 'Times' and 'Herald' put in by the wood companies.

February 9. Met John Laurie from New York in Portland Place and knew each other after 18 years.

10. Gave a dinner to Scrimgeour for his good management of the bank.

14. A grand debate in Sewers about wood, all in the 'Herald'.

21. Presided over 400 master tailors, a charitable dinner to erect almshouses for decayed journeyman tailors.

March 6. Lord Brougham having attacked the Corporation and me for extra-magisterial duties, Peter wrote a greatly admired reply signed P.L. in 'Times' this day. John Laurie left London for Edinburgh and New York.

11. Marlebone agreed by a majority of 4 *votes not* to lay down wood for 3 years.

16. A Scotch wedding at George Webster's *Reverend* Dr Buchanan.

April 18. Having by carefully examining all my affairs I found I was worth one hundred thousand pounds and had a new stall built for a 5th horse, and very ornamental to the garden. Considered this a memento of £100,000 realized property and thanked God for his goodness and considering my expences is wonderful and I beg to express my heartfelt gratitude for I have filled the expensive offices of sheriff, Lord Mayor, have always kept 4 horses since 1826,

had my summer rambles and have not forgotten my poor relations and been out of business since 29 September 1829, but I have never run risks by being eager for great interest, for when there are great gains there are always great risks.
27. Moved an address in Court of Aldermen to the Queen for her 2nd daughter.
May 1. The radicals of Marlebone put my name in their list and after 10 years I was again elected a vestryman of Marlebone, which was gratifying as I have always opposed them, but not voilently or vulgarly.
12. Friday, took the chair at Wesleyan public breakfast, London Tavern, room cranmed. Made a speech against the bishop of London and Puseyism, was greatly applauded. The speech in 'Times' and other papers and published in thousands at one penny each, bought and sent to every member of Common Council and also to several bishops and others who are[135] like myself, true Protestants.
17. A violent attack upon me in the 'Times' for my speech, saying I was mad upon that subject. Heggate elected chamberlain, Pirie unsuccessful, ought not to have started. Being a junior Heygate appointed the Union Bank his and the bank of the Corporation of London. 8 directors became 8 trustees for Heygate.
23. Consulted Mr Copeland, not well, gave me a blue pill.
27. In Mansion House report the Lord Mayor on the subject of shaving the prisoners said I must be on my way to Bethlem. Called and ask the Lord Mayor if he denied the words put in his mouth by the reporter. He said he was not answerable for newspaper reports. I told him they were the observations of a pompous, ignorant and vulgar man, left the office. He was more civil to me all the years afterwards. Lady Laurie and Miss Sparkes went to Tunbridge Wells.
29. Letters appeared in the 5 morning papers stating that the Lord Mayor repudiated the expressions attributed to him and the words I used also appeared and Mansion House report. Lady Laurie and Miss Sparkes returned having hired[136] appartments, and went back 3 June.
June 4. Went to Tunbridge Wells, returned 5.
8. Dined Albion, Aldersgate. Deputy Carrington in the chair.
17. Attended debate in vestry, motion to recind the minute of vestry not to pave with wood after a good and well conducted debate. For recinding 28, for ammendment not to pave with wood for 3 years 35, majority 15.
21. Lent a presentation to Christ's Hospital to George Forbes to be returned 1844.
23. House of Commons gave evidence against loans or swindly societies and Peter Laurie at the same time.
24. Proposed Moon for sheriff.
July 3. Bridwell annual dinner, very hot as usual. Had Sam Slick and Levato from U.S.
5. Tommy kicked, Regent's Park, obliged to sell him.
8. Went up with an address to the Queen.
11. Bought a new horse (£)60, got (£)15 for Tommy.

12. A most satisfactory meeting at the Union Bank, gave 5 per cent.
13. Bank directors dined Richmond.
29. Lady Mayoress's water party.
31. Reversionary dinner, Star and Garter.
August 6. Lady Laurie and I went to Brighton to look for a house, got none.
10. Dined on board the 'Bentick'.
11. Price, Adams and Frank Price started per railroad to Folkestone and Dover to view the Kentish estates and returned on Tuesday the 15 August.
18. Lady Laurie, Miss Wilkie *and I* started for Bath, Bristol, Clifton, Exeter, Torquay, Sidmouth, Weymouth, Bournmouth, Southampton, etc etc and returned 5 September. Torquay singular and beautiful.
September 11. Very hot. Peter returned from a 3 weeks trip to France.
October 10. Magnay returned after a poll against Wood and Humphrey.
11. Coachman with horses etc set of for Brighton. Lady Laurie and Miss Wilkie went to Brighton 9 October, 11, Royal Crescent, 10 guineas a week for a month.
15. Peter taken very ill at Bread Street wardmote. I came up from Brighton, Lady Laurie followed me on 17 and returned on 18th. Very cold.
November 20. After hunting etc left Brighton for London for the season.

Peter's pamphlet, a report of a committee of the Corporation recomending every one to be free without taking up his freedom and other great alterations in the Corporation. Peter at Brighton wrote a reply and observations upon the report. In my name sent the observations, printed by Spottiswood, to all members of the Corporation. Very clever and I believe saved the Corporation.
23. Carried every question against Wire and Pearson chiefly by Peter's pamphlet and my speech, he furnished me hints for it.
28. Got the Saddlers' Company to agree unanimously to all Peter's resolutions and sent them to other livery companies.
30. Proposed Canning for Scots' Hospital againts the free church people for Hamilton and beat them hollow.
December 18. The debate upon the Corporation's reform began on the 14, Thursday. I led on the debate and adjourned to the 18th when the division of the Court was against 113, for the report 54, majority 59, a quiet debate.
21. A wardmote and poll as usual. The late members chosen.
27. Lady Laurie and I stood godmother and godfather for Thomas Wilkie('s) daughter Helen.

1844.
January 8. Wilkie committee met. Lord Mahon in the chair made a final settlement and paid Joseph (£)750.
11. George Laurie from America dined with us.
14. Took possession of 3 sittings at Scobells, very touching.
February 1. Obtained orders for George Laurie and myself to see the Queen

open Parliament. Got a good place in the House of Lords.
18. Wrote to Mr Bonham that the Conservative Club was enough for me and declined being a candidate for the Carlton, but very much obliged by Lord Granville Somerset and Mr Bonham for proposing and seconding my nomination.
March 13. O'Connell's attack upon me at the Corn League, Covent Garden, not worth replying to. It was revenge because I would not allow him to be heard at opening Blackwall railway.
24. Peter asked me if I had any objections for him to marry Fanny Hulbert, that her fortune was (£)10,000 stock. I said if he liked her I could have no objection as it was a respectable family, yet with his expections he might have looked higher, but I was perfectly satisfied and he went on. The Hulberts were, as I said, delighted.
April 13. Collected all the documents respecting wood pavement to Mr Hume M.P. to move, which he did in the House of Commons, for the expence of Regents Street. This had the desired effect. Williams M.P. and I requested an interview with Lord Lincoln and the Committee of Woods and Forests. They wrote they would lay down no more wood for 12 months.
19. Agreed with Dr Beattie to take No. 6 for Peter's new house.
25. Queen's drawing room, very full.
May 2. Declined dining at the Mansion House to meet the bishops as they are generally a worthless set.
7. Attended the Bank of England meeting and shortly supported Peel's Bank Bill.
12. Westleyan breakfast. Took the chair at a meeting of this most respectable body. When I was asked by the deputation to preside, I said I had not read much of their proceedings but I would attack the bishop of London and the Puseite party in the church. They said nothing could be more acceptable to them, and I made a speech. The 'Times' said, who reported it fully 13 May, that I was mad. Thousands of this speech was sold at one livery. I sent one to every member of the Corporation and to the Bishop of Winchester and others[137].
14. Made a good speech against amalgamating the courts of Lord Mayor and the 3 court in Court of Aldermen against the plans of Pearson. A good report of speech 15 May.
15. A splendid dinner at Mansion House instead of Easter Monday.
23. Spoke in Common Council against opening the Lord Mayor's court, floored it with the aid of Low and Jones.
25. Dined with the judges, Mansion House.
26. Attended St Paul's, judges' sermon.
28. Gave a dinner to the Union Bank directors and officers, after going with Adams to see property at Hadesden.
June 2. Met the Emperor of Russia and King of Saxony in Piccadilly.
4. Moved that the Corporation present an address to Russia and Saxony, but

finding that Mr R. Taylor, Hall etc intended to oppose it, the Lord Mayor very properly declined to call a court such was the democratic feeling against the Emperor of Russia for his conduct to the Poles.
8. The North British board in London having been called upon to answer a Bill in Chancery and my name being necessary I discovered for the first time that Mr Boyd had taking proceedings against the Irish Agricultural Society without bringing it before the board. I was very angry. All particulars were sent to the Edinburgh board, they sanctioned it and I was satisfied, but added Mr Sewell's name to conduct the suit.
10. Went over Bethlem with the King of Saxony, then went to Rowfant, Hulbert's country seat, the introduction before the wedding.
13. Took possession of No. 6, Park Square to get No. 7 thoroughly painted.
16. Declined attending a charity sermon at Aldersgate Street unless the preacher, Dr Stebbing, preached in black, which he consented to do.
18. Attended the marriage of Dr Hunter with Miss Wilkie at Thomas Wilkie's. Then went and got the King of Saxony and the Lord Mayor to attend the opening and uncovering the statue of the Duke of Wellington, Royal Exchange.
24. Alderman Hunter and Mr Sidney chosent sheriffs.
30. Bishop of Salisbury preached the annual sermon for Bethlem hospital, a poor preacher.
July 3. Attended the funeral of Campbell the poet in Westminster Abbey. Present Peel, Brougham, Capper and about 200 mourners.
5. Attended Duchess of Buccleuch's breakfast from 3 to 7, all the fashionable world there, felt pleased with the invitation, had been there before but then as Lord Mayor, this is a compliment to myself. Regretted that Lady Laurie was too ill to accept the invitation.
10. Meeting of the Union Bank. A satisfactory meeting and 4 of the directors went out according to the deed and were all reelected by acclamation and I and Spottiswoode were reelected chairman and deputy chairman.
18. Mr Hulbert having agreed to give (£)10,000 stock with his daughter, he left the transfer receipt with Lady Laurie for £10,000, 3 per cent consols. I having agreed to whatever sum Mr Hulbert gave to Peter Laurie and this day transferred 4000 3%s to his name with other sums and house making the amount more than Mr Hulbert gave and I never gave any gift with greater pleasure as Peter deserved all I could give him.
20. Peter elected *unanimously* a guardian for Marlebone. Met the Nelson committee and transferred all out balance *to* the government who undertook to finish the pillar etc. Thus we got rid of a very troublsome but honorable job.
31. Lady and Laurie and I went to Rowfant, dined and slept.
August 1. This day was at the wedding of Peter Laurie and Fanny Hulbert. The service was performed by the rector the Reverend Mr Bethune. After lunch Peter and his wife set of for a tour of Ireland. I hope they will be happy.
2. Returned with Lady Laurie to London.

8. Lady Laurie, Miss Jack and Miss Nicol went to Broadstairs. I went 10 and returned 20.
24. Went to Ramsgate, remained till 1 September when I returned to propose Alderman Brown as chamberlain. He had 2 opponents, Sir John Key who has a very bad character deservdly so and Mr Humphrey, both given in first day but Mr Heppel kept the poll open to annoy Brown and had only 67 votes and Brown 2300. Brown continued to bank with the Union Bank for my kindness to him.
September 7. Went with Mr Price, Mr Adams, took my footman to Cheltenham then viewed the Oxfordshire property belonging to Bethlem.
10. Lady Laurie and Miss Sparkes returned from Ramsgate and Lady Laurie and Miss Nicol went again to Ramsgate.
17. Brown gave a grand dinner to his friends.
29. Gibbs and Wood returned by the livery and to our, the Aldermen's, (surprise) no poll demanded and we elected the least unpopular man, Gibbs, 12 to 6.
October 5. A great victory. I got by a vote in vestry for taking up wood and putting down granite in Oxford Street. I was considered mad for my opposition to wood and now I was the wise man. Let no man despair if in a minority if he is sane, he is right.
10. The King of the French having arrived at Windsor on a visit to the Queen, Alderman Humphrey moved and I seconded an address in the Court of Aldermen, was adopted by the Common Council, and on Saturday the 12 a deputation of Aldermen and Common Council, in all 30 presented an address to the King of the French, who said to Sir C. Hunter, 'ah, Sir Peter Laurie, I am glad to see you.' Hunter said 'that is Sir Peter', pointed to me, the King, 'ah, Sir Peter, I dined with you at the Fishmongers' Company.' After a lunch from the Queen we returned to London, all much gratified.
15. David Salomon having been returned as alderman from Portsoken ward, he presented himself to be sworn in, but in a long speech objected to sign the declaration 'upon the true faith of a Christian'. I replied, and the court rejected him 13 to 6 and a new writ was issued and Moon was elected unopposed. The Queen having agreed to open the Royal Exchange on the 28 in full state and I having urged the aldermen and 12 Common Councilmen to ride as a mounted guard nearest the Queen's state carriage, I had to (bring to) conclusion arrangements and after daily intercouse with the Adjutant General, Master of the Ordnance, visiting Woolwich, the procession did take place. 14 aldermen and 12 Common Council and all went of well without any mistake or accident, what is in the narration presented by me to the Court of Aldermen.
9. Lord Mayor's Day, few great men at the dinner.
29. A grand dinner was given to me by the gentlemen the mounted guard at Masons' Hall, Anderton in the chair. All thankful for my getting them quiet horses and enabling them to get fame and no ridicule.
December 5. The Coal, Corn and Finance committee reported to the Common

Council that they agreed to give (£)200 for a free church in St Giles's. I opposed it as it might be Puseyite clergyman and condemned in very strong terms the very arrogant and turbulent conduct of Bishop Phillpotts and the trimming, 'split-the-difference' Bishop Bloomfield. I was seconded by deputy Corney, who with the others the parishoners of Tottenham, from Bloomfield conduct the debate was adjourned and much praise and much blame heaped upon me by the newspapers.

12. Common Council. The debate resumed by a speech from the chairman of the committee and answered by Mr Wire in a great speech. So unanimous was the Court they would give no other member an opportunity of speaking and my amendement to postpone the consideration of the report for 12 months was carried 150 to 3. This is the greater blow the anti—protestants could have had and the greatest victory for the laity. The effect of this vote was astonishing in the country. The result of the whole was that the Bishops of Exeter and London withdrew their orders for the surplice.

14. The newspapers praised me except the 'Morning Post', the Puseyite, abused me daily for weeks after, said I led on the dance of the laity. Mr Hoare the banker in a speech attacked the bishops as firmly as I did but we were amply repaid by the result. 19. Dickens in his annual Christmas tale[138] this year introduced me as Alderman Cute, reolved to put down everything connected with the poor, because I, in 1841 I put down suicide by sending two persons for trial. The fact was in two months there were 23 attempts at Blackfriars Bridge, pathos and pity only seemed to increase the evil. The grand jury found a Bill, they were convicted and for the two following months, November and December instead of being 23 only two Napoleon, and other persons in power were obliged to render the attempt infamous to check it. The newspapers gave my name, but all abused the tale as setting the poor against the rich and it was in all reviews condemned except the *Edinburgh review*. It was dramatised and brought out at the Adelphi and Lyceum but was not successful and the alderman's put down produced no effect. This was the more disgraceful for Dickens as I had taken his wife to the Lord Mayor's dinner and was upon terms of civility with home, he is a dangerous man to meet. I was greatly hurt at the circumstances but I soon forgot it.

Peter wrote an excellent letter to the editor of the 'Literary Gazette' which Mr Jerdan, the editor, inserted with many very judicous remarks. This is the penalty all public men pays, particularly those who have made their own *fortune*. On the 20th at Aldersgate ward at the annual election for Common Council, they voted a vote of thanks to the Corporation for the vote they gave against Puseyismers, also a vote recommending no more wood pavement. Both these subjects I have ever opposed and these votes were most gratifying to me.

1845.

January. Lady Laurie still very unwell and confined to her room.

4. The Wellington committee met and viewed the statue which I secured to Chantrey and directed that 'Wellington' should be on each side and on the ends erected 'June 18, 1844'.

7. Gave Sir W. Magnay a direct appointment for a cadie to India to receive one in return from Sir W. Magnay.

10. Proposed and secured Price's son a seat in the Chartered Gas.

18. A great day at the vestry, Penfold having taken £25 as his own instead of giving it to the school. The sermon was preached for the school. I got him in the vestry to give up the £25.

25. Complained in the vestry of the reckless expenditure of the Middlesex magistrates and produced a great effect and reported in newspapers.

28. Sewers, City 10 to 6 against wood paving.

February 7. Summoned upon a jury. The Town Clerk sent Henry Welton, who pleaded my priviledge as an alderman and allowed.

25. W.M.Nurse's horse came down on Regents Street wood pavement and broke his leg.

March 6. Supported Locke for pleader against Sir W. Riddell. Lock 111, Riddell 91, in consequence of Gurney's retiring and giving Peter Laurie a step.

7. *Bethlem committee.* Lord Shaftesbury and the committee agreed to separate the offices of solicitor and clerk. I started Welton as candidate for clerk and agreed to support Still for solicitor.

9. Attended Christ's Hospital. The Queen and Prince Albert attended the supping.

11. Court of aldermen. Lord Mayor complained of his place as at the head of the royal hospitals being usurped.

24. A capital letter in the 'Times' written by Peter Laurie upon Brougham's Bill.

April 3. Peter Laurie sat for his picture to Mr Aloux. The King of the French having determined to have a picture of the address presented to him at Windsor sent Mr Aloux to take the 42 portraits and nothing could exceed the likenesses, they were done in water colour to be transferred to canvass in Paris.

4. I sat for my portrait. Everyone thought all the likenesses good but his own.

7. Welton elected clerk and Still, solicitor.

17. Gave according to our City custom a dinner to Mr Aloux at the Albion.

22. The Lord Mayor and aldermen accompanyed the Queen and Prince Albert to see the 'Great Britain' steamship, Blackwall. Margaret Laurie *11 years of age* daughter of Andrew Laurie came as an adopted daughter to Lady Laurie, saild from Leith, 19.

24. The humbug 'Needle Women's Society' zealously opposed by me in Common Council and rejected.

May 2. Went with a deputation to Lord Ashley's then to the drawing room, *not* crowded, got home ¼ before 4.3. Peter Laurie elected a vestryman of Marlebone, votes 192, Hamilton 143. This was very gratifying to me, a proof that both he and I were much respected by the liberals in Marlebone and confirmed, Monday 5.

April 27. Took young Margaret all over the Botanic zoological gardens and was much astonished at her intelligence and observation. She must have had able instruction added to her natural talents. This should have been 27 April.

May 6. A grand turn up at the Court of Aldermen. I condenned the sheriffs and praised the House of Lords for their noteing the disgraceful proceeding at the execution of Hacker.

10. Peter took his seat in the vestry.

19. New bank premisess opened, 2, Princes Street, Mansion House.

20. A very important trial of strength between Mr Price, the treasurer and me took place. He never was straightforwarded but now he supported Nisbett for apothcary, I took up Wood. Wood 100, Nisbett 43. Such a victory as he will never forget.

June 2. Prince Albert having agreed to come to the Hall Bridewell, to take his charge, on Saturday last when a deputation waited upon him at Buckingham Palace, he accordingly came and we received him in great state. The Lord Mayor came as Chief of the hospital took the chair, which he immediately gave up to 139
me, the president, as had been arranged and I delivered an address etc and the ceremony was very imposing, and a good account in the 'Herald', 3 June.

4. A Court of Aldermen. The Lord Mayor drank, as it is called, or rather named 9 liverymen for sheriffs, John Laurie being one.

10. Lady Laurie rode out for the first time since her confinement in November.

12, 13, 14 and 15. Intolerably hot.

16. Margaret Laurie went to Miss Maine's for one week, who wrote to Mrs Lough that Margaret was remarkably clever.

23. Lady Laurie, Peter, Margaret and Anne went by the train to the York Hotel where apartments had been secured by letter. Horses and chariot and coachman went at the same time but not by rail.

24. Alderman Challis and John Laurie had agreed to serve sheriffs some months ago, but Mr Challis wished to have his brother-in-law Mr Kennard and John's serving was postponed. And Challis and Kennard were by everyone considered concluded, but Mr Wire who was to be John's under sheriff, started at the hour of election Chaplin and Laurie and got his friends and adherents to come and hold up their hands. They had the majority and were to our great astonishment declared sheriffs. John wrote to Challis and said he knew nothing about the matter. A most unexpected event.

26. Went to Brighton and returned on Saturday.

29. The Bishop of Lichfield preached. *Sermon* was amusing.

30. A court, Bridewell.

July 2. The grand dinner, 150 dined. A good account in the 'Herald', went off

capitally, mentioned the great merit of Dr Webster and Mr Laurie in drawing up their able report.
3. Dined with a friend I had known 40 years the chief baron Pollock. I lived with his father and we were boys together 45 years ago.
4. Went to Brighton, very ill on Saturday and Sunday and for days afterwards.
7. Returned from Brighton.
8. Not well but still went to the Bank dined evening *with* Peter Laurie with Dr Lee and his son.
9. A glorious day for our Union Bank, no success equal to this. A good account in 'Herald'. Shares increased in value from 10 to 13.
10. Dinner given to Scrimgeour by the bank at the London Tavern.
11. Went to Brighton to see Lady Laurie, returned the 15.
21. Lord Mayor's party, the barge. Lord Bishop of London there, and cut me for my antipuzite speech.
31. Attended Reversionary society, all went off well. Attended afterwards the Common Council always complained of the usurped power of the Lord Mayor to keep a court by locking the door. I saw the Lord Mayor desire the sword bearer to give him the key which he put in his pocket. I then walked quietly to the bottom of the court, stooped under the prison bar, turned round and told the Lord Mayor I was not upon the rota and would not be detained or locked in by anyone and retired. Anderton said, 'my Lord Mayor, there is no court'[140]. I congratulated by the members as the only one that had courage to break up the petty tyranny, and am astonished that the members submitted it. At a Court of Common Council a motion by Mr Lot to take my conduct into consideration and which was held 25 September when Mr Storms Hale jumped near the bar and put an end to the farce.
August 1. Set off with Peter Laurie and Mr Adams to Lincolnshire, had all the tenants to pay their rent as usual. John Wood joined us at the hall on the 6, returned home on the 7, slept at Huntingdon, and came home by Cambridge.
9. Got to Brighton returned the 12 to dine with the East India Company, 13.
14. Started with Peter and Fanny for France, a 2½ (hour) passage from Folkstone. Slept Hotel de Bains, hired an open carriage from Hotel de Bord. Slept at Abbevile, and got to Paris 16, a 15 hours journey. Went to Hotel de Bristol. Went to Versailes 17, Sunday afternoon and the first sympton of a boil which became very troublesome as will hereafter be mentioned. Remained in Paris till Friday the 22, came by coupe diligence to Boulogne and on Saturday slept Folkstone. Came to London 24 and went to Brighton 25. All the particulars in Letts' dairy, was unwell and did not enjoy my journey at all. Hot in Paris.
25. Went to Brighton and returned 27, returned to Brighton 26(?), not well. Lay upon the sofa, 1, Royal Crescent and could not walk, in great pain.
September 2. Consulted Mr Copeland, Cavendish Square, found an abscess or tumor on the side of the anus, ordered leeches.

3. Gave Scrimgeour a piece of plate and dinner, invited his friends London Tavern. All went off well, I was in pain.
4. Copeland allowed me to go to Brighton with a mackintosh, Copeland air cushion.
8. Peter and Fanny arrived at Brighton from Dieppe.
10. I returned from Brighton.
12. Copeland ordered more leeches and would not allow me to go to Brighton, remained on the sofa 12 days.
23. Lady Laurie and little Margaret returned from Brighton. Lady Laurie no better, had a chair made to carry her up and down stairs. Could not do my duty Guildhall nor to see the sheriff sworn in, 27.
29. Ill as I was I went to do my duty at the Court of aldermen to keep out Wood. 14 voted for Johnson and 7 for Wood. The livery ought not to have returned Wood. My object is to get honest aldermen and keep out rogues.
30. In very great pain yet I was obliged to dine with the sheriffs at their inaguration dinner on John's account. A company much too numerous.
October 1. Mr Copeland lanced my boil and desired lintseed poulties 4 or 5 times a day. Persevered in this treatment and Mr Groom was an excellent nurse.
2. Margaret went to Miss Maine's school.
9. Peter and Fanny went with Lady Laurie to Bath. Slept at Swindon and reached Bath 10th.
20. This day Mr Copeland and Mr Wade called and operated upon me for a fistula, the cutting painful but not long duration, very little blood. Had a bed put up in library, went to bed where I remained 7 days, 28, when I came into dining room for one hour on the sofa. On 29 dressed for the first time was calm and not fretful. Read *nearly* all Scott's novels over again and they were more entertaining than at first reading. The doctors called daily, and got well rapidly.
November 5. Went into the City, Bank etc.
6. Called and gave Copeland £20. Was obliged to take to the sofa again and not so well.
9. Not well enough to go to the Lord Mayor's dinner. Remained quiet, Wade coming almost every day.
19. Called and gave Wade 10 guineas. On the 15 spoke against the Regent's canal railway.
22. Slept in my own bedroom, 2d floor, after 5 weeks sleeping in library.
27. Went to Bath, 3 Paragon, where Lady Laurie had been since 9 October. Found her very little better under the advice of Mr Norman, bathing etc etc.
December 1. Returned to London. A frost.
4. Slipt up, the ice being on the steps and great pain in the side and wrist. Lay in bed and had a douche bath by Thomas pouring hot water every hour on my wrist.
9. The dispute about the Corporation fixing seals to the hospital deeds, agreed to do so, 2 to 1.

11. Went with Margaret to Bath.
15. Returned from Bath. Carried a book to sit on in the railway carriages.
22. Wardmote, all the members elected. A vote against the Corn Laws etc.
25. Went to Bath Christmas day. The train carriages empty. Guards ashamed of it. During my confinement the railways mania prevailed and I was glad I had the prudence to withhold my name from all. Then came the panic. Peter was as prudent as (blank).
31. This was a most unfortunate year to me, I was laid upon the sofa and deprived of my walking and riding from 1st September, being the only year I ever had above two or three days illness.

1846.
January 5. Left Bath by train. Mrs Bedford brought James Kedslie, a short boy, put him into Christ's Hospital.
20. My complaint not gone, in morning gown 2 *or 3* days.
27. Rode round the Regent's Park for the 1st time for months. The failure of Emanuels, Samuels, Linnet etc gave us all much pain and a slight run on the bank, but it was all over in 2 days.
30. *Peter* went to[141] Bath to bring up Lady Laurie.
31. They all returned, Lady Laurie in good spirits and a little better.
February 3. Summer weather. Not able to sit on a soft sead and carried a book with me to sit on. Attended all City and vestry meetings as usual.
March 4. Peter went to Frankfort on bank business to secure some of Emanuel property from the grasp (of?) Roshilid, and succeeded.
11. Came home to meet Kid. He came an hour before I came home. Desired Lady Laurie not to move and put on splints.
17. Attended Sewers, City. 40 present, 39 for stone and 1 for wood viz Mr Eagleton. 2 years ago 39 for wood and 1 for stone, that one myself. This paragraph went the round of the newspapers.
19. Queen's drawing room, went but very thin.
April 2. The inspectors having in their report stated many falsehoods to the Home Secretary respecting Bridewell, a committee was apointed and their report was approved of. Had it printed and sent to the governors and a written copy and letter sent to Sir James Graham.
6. When the freedom of the City was voted to General Nott and General Sale 4 years ago, General Sir George Pollock was not included. Mr Jones called upon me respecting voting the freedom to Sir H. Harding and General Gough. I approved of it and gave notice to the town clerk of my intention to propose the freedom to Sir George Pollock. I felt a great unwillingness to get support as this victories were in 1842, but I persevered and brought on my motion after the others had been carried and stated that the vote was not brought forward in 1842 because he was not in England and the other generals were. I further stated I knew all the Pollocks' boys and it gave me heartfelt satisfaction to have the honor

and privilege of, after 40 years *friendship* proposing a vote of the freedom of London to *the sons of* one of the most honorable men that ever lived and it was gratifying to see one son chief baron, another a queen's council and then the hero of Hyber Pass, Sir George Pollock; carried my notion of the freedom in a gold box of 100 guineas by acclamation.

13. This day my niece Mrs Richards died. When I came to London her house was my home, at least I dined almost every Sunday in Holborn where her husband, a clever man, lived, and for above 40 years we reamined in an unterrupted friendship. Mr Richards died *1840 October* and was buried Highgate cemetry. Mrs Richards was buried in the same grave, 18 April. Mrs Richards had more wisdom than almost any woman I ever saw, was 9 years confined to her small house, was independent in mind and in circumstances and although very limited, never complained. She was my own age and never was a brother and sister more attached than we were. Her strength of mind, contentment under all circumstances, and she had her *severe* trials, never were surpassed and I and Lady Laurie most severely felt her loss. She died at the same age of her husband, 68. She was the daughter of my oldest brother whom I never saw.

10. Sunday. Rode this day quietly about the new buildings in Marlebone and saw with disgust the fair at Chalk Farm with swings, roundabouts and donkey races. I brought the subject before the Marlebone vestry, stated I had mentioned the subject to the St Pancras magistrates, they could do nothing. My speech was reported in the 'Times' and the Home Secretary gave orders to the police and all was removed by the next Sunday. This will shew what one man can do in a just cause, it gave great satisfaction.

21. Carried an address to the King of the French upon his escape from the assassin, Lecomter.

22. Ministers' dinner at the Mansion House. As the senior alderman I returned thanks and said we were attached to our rights and privileges and nothing could divert us from them and we would resist the attempt of the government, regardless of who was minister.

23. Common Council agreed with the Court of Aldermen's address.

May 1. Peter and Fanny went to Brussels by Ramsgate for a week.

This day sent a pamphlet, 'Killing no murder', written by Peter Laurie but sent out under my name. This pamphlet was occasioned by the inspectors of prisons' report where they laud the seperate system of imprisonment. This has ever been considered by me and Mr Laurie as the most cruel and infamous of treatment and a more able statement and refutation of such opinions never was penned. I sent it to the great officers of state, the judges and had answers from some of the judges and others. It made a great sensation at the Home Office and at Reading goal which it attacked with severitey and justice.

22. The Lord Chief Baron, my old friend, Sir H. Wilton, General Robertson, Mirehouse dined.

23. This day my old complaint returned and I was in such pain I sent for Wade.

Leeched and I was in very great pain till Tuesday morning when I sent for Mr Copeland and they lanced the part and a very great discharge took place which gave me immediate ease. Lay on the sofa for 3 weeks and slept in the library all the time, Charles putting on poultices 3 or 4 times a day. Copeland came 4 times, Wade 25. June 12, gave Copeland £5, Wade £12 12(s), Charles 20/- and slept upstairs and pronounced well, but not to ride for a week.

June. Very hot, very hot all the month.

13. At vestry brought forward the subject of advertising bans. Agreed to appoint a chairman, Manners, and a deputation to see Sir James Graham.

24. Challis and Kennard chosen sheriffs. The sheriffs Chaplin and Laurie gave the judges a dinner at the Crown and Sceptre, Greenwich at my suggestion, and greatly approved.

25. Ibrahim Pasha made a great noise as a lion here dined with the Queen, was canvassed by everyone, dined with the Lord Mayor, yet a mere savage. He with his suite some pasha, Col. Bonforth, Nubar and Major Dickson went over Bethlem and were astonished at the lunatic working at various trade like sane persons.

27. The aldermen 7 to 6 agreed to go to Oxford. I moved they should not go beyond Staines, seconded by Duke but lost. And on Mon(d)ay 20 July the Court of Common Council, moved by Anderton and seconded by me that the Corporation do not pay the Lord Mayor's expences out of the jurisdiction, against Laurie, Duke and Wood, for going to Oxford Wilson, Marshall and Sidney.

July 8. The annual meeting at the Union Bank as we had met with great losses, some[142] expected a stormy meeting, I did not. Although many questions were asked, all went off well. Elected Charles Lyall a director.

20. Peter had a daughter born this day.

25. Court of Aldermen. Wilson moved a protest against the Common Council, I counted out the Court.

August 1. A dreadful thunder storm.

8. Objected to go to Oxford with the Lord Mayor, not being in his jurisdiction, but on Saturday the 8 the Conservancy went and took Miss's Hunters.

21. Peter had his daughter christned Beatrice Margaret.

25. Artificial teeth a great blessing had them put in by Mr Saunders, does admirably. Gave him 10 guineas after he made great alterations.

September 1. I added a codicil to my will and substituted D. Webster with his own consent for A. Thomson as trustee and executor. Thomson to my great regret going to reside in Coldstream instead of London.

2. 'Times Testimonial' dinner. My old complaint having returned leeched on the 2d and opened with a lancet 3d. Painful.

3. Lady Laurie, Peter, Margaret set off for Buxton, slept at Derby. Peter returned from Buxton.

14. Mrs Laurie and child went to Wiltshire.

16. Having been attended by Mr Wade from the 3 to the 16 September, gave him 10 guineas being quite well.
17. Went to Derby, slept at hotel and then next day went by mail to Buxton. Found Lady Laurie the same as to former complaints, but her sprain from the overturn of the chair much worse than I expected. Remained at Buxton 5 days, then met the Lord Mayor Farebrother at Hull, 24, on 25 to Brandsburton viewed the farms etc. Left Brandsburton 26, got to London 27. Attended Court of Aldermen 28 and the election of Lord Mayor 29. A poll demanded. Poll kept open till 8 October. Carroll 1653, Wood 1644, Carroll unanimously elected.
October 15. A great row Court of Aldermen about the Oxford trip.
23. I went with Price, Peter Adams, Smirke and Wilton to Kent to view the farms. All satisfied, no complaints, no famine. Returned by 27.
November 2. Dined with Carroll, inaguration, very hot. My complaint returned, another abcess, could not be with riding as I have not rode since 1 September. Wade leeched me 6 November and lanced abcess Monday.
9. A great relief. Could not go to Guildhall, Lord Mayor's Day. Went on leeching till the 13 November when Mr Copeland operated upon me a second time and the treatment was as before and after being confined to my bedroom etc, went 4 December to Brighton, 13, Crescent.
December 17. Conflict between the Lord Mayor advised Recorder began Carroll refusing to put a question or putting a notice on the business paper. I was the only alderman that agreed with the Common Council.
21. Wardmote. Unanimous thanks after my supporting the Common Council.
31. Had a committee of inhabitants at my house to oppose the Regent's canal railway.

1847.
January 1. Very cold and sleet.
6. Returned from Brighton. Lady Laurie returned 9 January.
23. Rode first time since 31 August 1846.
25. Bridewell court. Morley's mothion to deprive us of our privilege of nominating, carried unanimously against him.
February 3. Grand row Common Council, Lord Mayor as ass, met almost weekly and the same result.
March 2. Lord Morpeth said in the House of Commons that the Crown should not consent to the railway Regent's Park.
18. A rash on my face, not well, called in Wade, could not shave for some time.
April 18. Commemoration. Bishop Oxford. Capital.
May 9. Elected vestryman for 3 years. An attempt to keep out conservatives.
12. Ministers' dinner, Mansion House.
15. Opposed building washhouses. Vestry very hot.
20. Dr Lauder and Mr Wade consult about Miss Jack, orderd her to remain in bed.

22. A row in vestry about my speech respecting the nasty custom of 20 or more naked fellows in plunging bath.
23. Judges at St Paul's.
June 17. Saw Mr Melville about Sir George Pollock.
21. Lady Laurie, Margaret, Ann and Thomas with carriage went by 12 o'clock train to Derby for Buxton.
22. They went to Buxton and I returned to London.
July 14. A very satisfactory meeting Union Bank. The consequence was shares got up to 13½.
23. Peter went off and remained two days at Derby and returned 25.
29. Election. Voted for Johnson and Beavan, wrote to committee and said why I could not vote for Masterman and Freshfield as they wish to alter the criminal law.
30. Marlebone election. Voted for Hamilton.
August 1. Went to the Italian opera, Covent Garden. Intolerably hot.
5. Mr Adderley's will. Mr Small wrote a note, says Mr Adderley died 2d August and left us £500 a piece. Did not think he meant me but Mr Small and his son called August 6 at Saddlers' Hall. They knew nothing of the will.
10. Went to Buxton to join Lady Laurie. Slept at Derby, remained at Buxton till Tuesday the 17. Received a letter from Mr Trenow and W. Brass, executors to Mr Adderley's will stating that he had left me £500. John and Peter had letters saying he had left them £150 each, also all the Saddlers' Court had legacies. This was very kind in Mr Adderley and very unexpected by us as there was no great intimacy, only he also said he approved of my conduct as a magistrate.
17. Scotland. Lady Laurie, Margaret, and I with 2 servants and barouche left Buxton, slept at Sheffield, put the carriage on the rail. Slept Darlington, Berwick and reached Edinburgh Friday, 20. Secured apartments Mackay's Hotel.
24. Tuesday. Leaving Lady Laurie and Margaret at Mackay's, took Andrew, Margaret's father, with me. Went to Perth, slept Blair Authol, then Inverness, Elgin, Aberdeen, Montrose, Arbroath, Leslie and reached Edinburgh August 31. A rought short account, I have written in Letts diary of this tour with remarks, not being necssay to copy them into this book.
September 3. Left Edinburgh, remained two days at Melrose, slept at Langholm, Carlisle, Liverpool, Birmingham, two nights at Coventry and got home 11 September. A short account also in Letts diary. I was from 10 August to the 11 September from (home). Very delighted with our tour after we had returned home and forgot our inconvenices consequent upon travelling and glad, very glad that our fated residence was London.
14. Peter and his wife returned after being at Vienne, Prague, Munich etc, having left London 4 August. John and his son John left London (blank) day, went to Hanover, Berlin, Hamburgh. People traveling mad and foolish, they had better stay at home and save their money.

25. Engaged Miss Heaton to come as a daily governess to Margaret at 5/- a day or £6 a month.

The Lord Mayor, *G. Carroll*, and Lady Mayoress called and asked if the 9th October would be a suitable day for the dinner to the Duke of Cambridge and our coach tickets. I said a very proper day. I had before told the Lord Mayor he could not get his vote of thanks unless we had a dinner for our coach tickets.

29. Hooper unanimously elected Lord Mayor.

October 9. Grand dinner, Mansion House, Duke of Cambridge there and Mr Brook(e) of Borneo there.

21. Carried a motion Common Council for Brooke to have the freedom of the City.

29. Brooke received his freedom.

November 9. Dined at Guildhall.

16. Carried a vote of thanks to Sir G. Carroll in the Court of Aldermen unanimously.

18. Vote of thanks refused to Sir G. Carroll in the Common Council, two to one.

27. Received from the late Mr Adderley executors £482 10s, amount of legacy deducting 3½ per cent. Had a bad cold.

December. Lady Laurie's last illness[143]. I now approach one of the most painful and distressing events of my life, viz the last illness of my dear wife.

3. Lady Laurie not well, not able to come down to dinner as usual. She had been carried down to dinner for nearly two years.

4. Mr Wade called in.

7. Peter, Fanny and I went to Covent Garden theatre, Shakespere night to raise a fund for buying Shakespere's house. When away Lady Laurie took a bleeding at the nose and sent for Wade at 10 o'clock, at ½ past 11 when I came home she was asleep. Wade called daily.

12. Wade put on 10 leeches and was here 4 times that day.

14. Wade twice a day, Lady Laurie worse and worse.

17. Lady Laurie now dangerously ill, called in Dr Watson, I remained now at home alarmed.

19. Lady Laurie a little better. Mrs Cox came to be with her a most excellent and good woman, Lady Laurie's great favorite. Called upon the Lord Mayor who agreed to preside at my wardmote on Tuesday if Lady Laurie was not worse.

21. Held the wardmote myself and from the uncertain state of Lady Laurie's health it was all over in an hour, not being certain if Lady Laurie was alive upon my return.

24. Lady Laurie a little better and we had new hopes. Had nurses from Mr Sparkes' and John Laurie's. Mrs Cox still here and most attentive.

30. Lady Laurie very ill and not expected to live. Had Dr Watson *again* who gave no hopes.

31. A melancholy close of the year 1847.

1848.

January 1. Mrs Cox, Peter and Fanny up all night, Wade hourly.

2 and 3. All again up both nights, never leaving the bedside of Lady Laurie who was not in pain.

4 **and** 5. All up still and the same unvareing attention, great grief and suffering in all of use, Peter, Margaret and Mrs Cox never left the bedside, giving nourishment.

6. Still the same but at 7 o'clock Margaret gave a shriek, we all went to the bedside, Mrs Cox, Peter Laurie, Fanny, Margaret, Mrs Robert, al(l) saw one of the very best of women fall asleep in Peter's arms. Oh what a scene, the first death bed I ever saw and can never be obliterated from my memory. *She* died on the very day we were married 6 January 1803, having been married 45 years. No one but those in the like circumstances can imagine the agony and this day Margaret Laurie my beloved wife died.

7. Had Mr Smith the undertaker and made all the arrangements for the funeral, to get a vault in Highgate cemetry. Peter gave all the necessary directions to Mr Machlacklin, Mrs Laurie to Miss Aitchison's, Miss Jack, all the Hunters etc etc and they all said they never saw to handsome a corpse, others said she looked like an angel. I did not move out of the house till the 13th, the day of the funeral. I was very unhappy, very unwell. Peter was completely knocked up, his exertions was above all praise. I had 140 letters of consolations and cards of enquiry.

13. **Funeral day.** At 10 o'clock a hearse and two mourning coaches with 4 horses each; 1(st) coach, self, Peter Laurie, John Laurie and Alexander Thomson, 2d coach, Mr Hulbert, Sir Chapman Marshall, Dr Hunter and Mr Maclauren. There was 4 private coaches, my own, John's, Mr Hulbert's and Mrs Ried, Sir George Carroll and others wished to send their carriages but was declined as we wished the funeral to be as plain as possible suitable to the good taste of my poor wife who disliked all ostentation.

15. Rode to Highgate and saw the grave and was well pleased with the situation.

18. Margaret and I dined together for the first time. Now are we blessed with a superintending providence. Margaret had been nearly three years with my wife, had the advantage of her instruction and pious example, kept all her accounts and I put the whole house under her care although not yet 14 years of age, and she conducts every thing to my entire satisfaction. I do not know what I should have done without her as I never did attend to the little house affairs and I made no change in my establishment, Mrs Peter Laurie undertaking to look in and aid Margaret when wanted, yet she requires little aid.

February 1. Margaret very unwell, called in Wade who came daily till the 19. Mrs Cox and Mrs Robert Laurie were each one week with Margaret till she got better. Distributed rings etc among my late wife's friends. Peter was very ill for 2 or 3 weeks, now better.

26. A ward meeting[144] Aldersgate to petition against the income tax. A republic in France.

28. Income tax additional given up.
March 9. Gave instructions for probate for Lady Laurie, Clark at Boyds valued her property at £4,924. Got the probate from Mr Farquher on Monday.
15. Lodged probate, will office Bank of England, Mr Smee and Mr Gray said they would transfer without a broker.
16. Spoke a little Bank of England, my spirits returning.
21. Moved an address Court of Aldermen on the birth of a princess.
23. Court of Common Council did not agree to our address, I did all I could to make them agree but in vain, and said if we did not agree no address would be received at the palace. Mrs Laurie went to Lowbridge for a month.
April 1. Warm for one week only.
3. Thomas Gray my brother-in-law died at Dolphinstone, 31 March, aged 85. Left a japanned box at Clarks with my name, painted 1848, containing my will.
8. Margaret's birthday aged 14, height 5ft 3(in). The Chartists having proclaimed to hold a meeting at Kennington Common, all London was in a stirr. Special constables were sworn in by thousands, 23,000 in the City, the artillery, the life guards etc all were in readiness, footguards in Bridwell, cavalry and artillery, House of Commons.
10. The meeting took place, Feargus O'Connor delivered up his colours and the petitions, went to the House of Commons in cabs and all was quiet by 4 o'clock.
13. Lord Hardinge received the freedom of the City dined at the Mansion (House). I could not go so early after my severe loss.
15. W. Lawrence elected alderman instead of Hughes, Hughes resigned being ruined by railway speculation.
17. Ralph Price having resigned as treasurer of Bridwell and Bethlem hospital, Mr Johnson was unamimously elected treasurer in his stead. A vote of thanks was proposed by Chamberlain Brown, seconded by Mr Deacon, carried, then John(son) proposed by Joseph Wilson, seconded by Mr Hail.
18. Heard a splendid speech by Peel, House of Commons, upon the Crown and Government Bill.
21. Good Friday, did not go to church, went Easter Sunday. Went 22, with Mr Thomson, Kew Gardens.
24. Margaret's first lesson Captain Hall. Did not go to the Easter Monday dinner.
26. Transferred all the funds in Lady Laurie's *name* in the Bank of England into my own name.
May 12. Went up with an address to the Queen on the birth of a child.
21. Margaret, 1st day on horseback, twice round the park.
28. Bethlem sermon, Bishop Worcester preached.
June 3. Went with Margaret to Tunbridge Wells to see Miss Jack.
9. Addiscombe examination etc, all very good.
27. Visited Mrs Hulbert.
28. Bridewell great dinner, Sir George Pollock and Bishop of Oxford present.

July 6. Went and saw Mrs Tripp's poney.
7. Bought poney £25 conditionally.
12. Bank meeting, dined at Richmond.
15. Dinner to Lord Shaftesbury, Grillion's.
17. At North British, at Blackwall.
21. Took Margaret first time to Conservatncy dinner up the river.
27. Reversionary meeting satisfactory.
August 1. Very sick and a red face.
2. Went to Wainfleet and returned Tuesday 8th.
9. Peter and Fanny and Miss Hulbert went to Germany.
12. Went to Marshall's, well fitted up, but very damp and unhealthy, returned Monday.
21. Lady Marshall died.
24. Went with Margaret and Ann Thomson to Southampton, then to the Isle of Wight, Portsmouth, Worthing, Brighton and returned on Monday 4 September.
September 5. Margaret's new governess came.
7. Miss Jack went to Ramsgate.
11. Peter, Fanny and Miss Hulbert returned in consequence of Mrs Laurie's severe illness.
16. Mrs Laurie called in Wade.
21. Margaret and John and Peter went to Stanmore to see child.
23. Went to Ramsgate to see Miss Jack and returned 25, Monday.
29. Peter wrote letters upon the reports of the commissioners which appeared in 'Chronicle' and 'Herald' in reply to Sidney. Sir James Duke elected Lord Mayor without any opposition.
30. John Laurie from New York came to London from Edinburgh. Dined with us Monday 2d October.
October 4. Took John Laurie to the Highgate cemetery to see my poor wife's grave.
5. Had a dinner party to meet John Laurie.
6. John Laurie left for Liverpool on his way to New York. A capital letter from Peter in 'Chronicle' in reply to a leading article.
17. Called Horse Guards, War Office ordnance, Mr Poynard, found Rotch told a lie as usual, they did not want Cold Bath fields as a barrack.
19. Peter 'dressed Rotch, Middlesex sessions, who withdrew his presentment.
24. Pony kicked in Hyde Park, John had to ride him, Mrs Laurie and child came to No. 6.
November 9. Tickets to Lyall.
11. Spoke against the separate system, greatly applauded.
13. A good account in 'Times' from observer of the vestry meeting.
18. A good hit in vestry.
27. Bridewell court, motion carried for treasurer not to have any nominations.

29. Attended Old Bailey sessions, my own sessions.
December 7. Margaret not well, visited with Mrs Laurie to Stowe.
14. Middlesex county meeting. Armstrong and Rotch moved to remove tread-wheel, Peter Laurie, Fresfield, Elliott and myself: for 2, against 34. Rotch removed from committee. Dined Merchant Tailors'.
21. St Thomas's, all Common Council reelected.

1849.
January 6. A grand field day, vestry memorials from Porcester and unions.
8. A meeting about new gaol, Aldersgate, a very small meeting as the funds to build were to come from the City cash. Resolved to give up the vain attempt to rouse the people.
9. A good report of Aldersgate meeting in all the papers.
12. Went with Mr Hume, Peter Laurie, Williams, was pleased with Western Bridewell, Millbank, disgusted with the house of detention, to Pentonville went in Hume's coach.
13. Attended Home Office, Sir George Grey, a public man, Hume beat him into fits.
15. Took down hatchmen, poor Lady Laurie had been dead and buried one year and 3 days. Put the servants in coloured clothes, but no joy, a sad, sad day with us *all*. Pearson's lecture not good. 2d night better.
18. Middlesex county meeting, Wilks withdrew his motion, a great victory. 16 memorials sent in against the expence, many of the(m) written by Peter Laurie.
20. Dined Saddlers' to meet other masters.
25. Cruickshanks came to take a portrait from Wilkie's painting for a locket for Margaret.
27. Pony behaved so ill resolved to sell him.
February 22. Attended leveée, not full, rode park afterwards.
28. Dined Mansion House, took Mrs Laurie.
March 1. Middlesex county meeting, a long discussion, Wilks withdrew his motion. I spoke about the sheepshearing. Peter as usual laid it into Rotch etc.
3. Sold pony to Mr Freeman for £25, the same I gave for him, the best pony in England.
15. Moved at the Bank of England a vote of thanks to governor, deputy governor and directors by acclamation.
19. A singular scene, Guildhall licencing day.
April 7. Went for a day or two to Romford, Marshall's.
9. Easter Monday, did not go.
16. A great victory Middlesex sessions against Rotch etc.
25. Dined Ministers' dinner, Mansion House at 8 o'clock. Sold Cornwall Terrace for (£)15,000.
30. Poynder as chaplain 97, Hooper 66, Wilde 6, Bridewell.
May 16. Dined Goldsmiths'.

19. Queen shot at by Hamilton. Left name at Buckingham House.
25. Declined dining with the judges, Mansion House, not well.
29. George Laurie from New York.
31. Mr Sparkes died.
June 1. Mrs Laurie and Miss Hulbert went to drawing room.
6. Mr Sparkes buried, St George's ground.
8. Mrs Robert Laurie and Margaret went to Scotland.
19. Mr George Laurie went to Scotland.
20. Mrs Robert's extraordinary letter from Edinburgh.
25. Mrs Robert and Margaret came by express from Edinburgh.
27. Bethlem dinner.
July 2. Lord John Manners stood for the City opposing Rothchild. Mr Baring proposed Lord John and I seconded. Rothchild returned again for the City.
11. An unanimous meeting, Union Bank.
20. Brown horse fell in the mews, a wonderful escape.
21. Conservancy up the river, Lord Mayor's party.
26. Meeting Rversionary, satisfactory.
27. Went to Kent to see property, Dover, Ramsgate, Margate and returned on Monday.
August 17. Unwell, called in Wade.
23. Went to Essex, Hale Bridge.
September 7. Went to Oxford, viewed the farms and returned 11th.
18. Went to christening of John's boy at Romford, Francis Duke, returned 19.
22. Went to Windsor, Peter, Fanny and Margaret, returned 25.
30. Opening Coal Exchange, a humbug, see Letts.
November 2. Went to Brighton, at York, etc to see Mrs John Laurie a visit.
5. Returned to London.
6. Put McPherson into Christ's Hospital. Miss Lina Kónig came to Margaret 2 days a week 7/- a day.
9. Dined Guildhall, had the Haigs.
December 2. Queen Dowager died.
4. I moved a vote of condolence, Court of Aldermen, seconded by Alderman Humphrey.
13. Queen Dowager buried.
21. Wardmote. Poll demanded by Alcock closed, Alcock only 47 votes.

1850.

January 15. Mrs Peter Laurie delivered of a son and heir at ½ past 3 o'clock.
29. Took the chair for the Watford Water company.
March 8. Peter Laurie resigned the pleadership in a letter to the Lord Mayor.
April 1. Margaret and John dined Easter Monday, was very ill in consequence.
May 1. Peter Laurie elected a director, North British and Reversionary Society.
2. A discussion upon seclar education. Mr Bennoch and Mr Willie proposed and

seconded, I moved the previous question seconded by Mr Matthews, Court counted out, they had no chance.
13. Went to Ware to please Mr Salisbury.
21. An opposition list for vestry. They did me the favour to be on both lists. Opposition list carried by a good majority. Peter Laurie in new list. New list 2565, old 2079, majority 486.
June 20. John Laurie from New York called.
29. Address to the Queen. Took Barbara and Agnes to see the procession in Pall Mall.
July 8. Vote of condolence to Mrs Peel in Common Council. Peel died 3 July.
10. Bank meeting very good. Black horse broke his knees.
15. Mansion House, proposed 1st resolution respecting the statue to Sir Robert Peel, a good meeting.
25. Peter Laurie elected on Saddlers' court. Peter and Fanny went to Wiesbaden for her tre(atment).
28. Miss Jack died, a very good woman.
August 1. Miss Jack buried with Lady Laurie, Highgate cemetry. Mourners W. Brownley, J. Laurie and A. Thomson.
8. Kent view with treasurer etc, 3 days.
28. My old complaint.
30. Great pain all night, Wade lanced the parts.
September 1. Operation. In bed upstairs until Sunday 15, Wade calling and dressing wound 3 times a day.
15. Down to dinner. Mrs Laurie came from Germany 17th.
18. Went to Bank, still in bed till midday.
21. Mrs Laurie with Peter came from Margate.
24. Much better. Went to the election of recorder, cleared the Court of Aldermen, for Stuart-Wortley 13, for Gurney 6. The election was carried to prevent Mr Gurney making a vacancy, which would have let in Mr Prendergast or Mr Locke, being judges at the Old Bailey. Wade called, took leave and I gave him £21.
28. Musgrove elected Lord Mayor.
30. Breakfasted downstairs first time.
October 1. Paid Mr Northall Laurie Miss Jack's balance.
9. Margaret, I and Thomas *Turner* left London ½ past 4 arrived Folkestone at 7, went on board at 10, left harbour at ¼ after 11, got to Boulogne at 2. Slept Bath Hotel, damp beds, caught a severe cold.
10. Mr and Mrs Northall Laurie arrived at 3. Dined and slept.
11. Paris. Left Boulogne at 12 after 12. Arrived at Paris at 6 at Meurice's, dark and dismal apartments.
12. Drove about Paris, dined Labb de Lot, good and cheerful.
14. New apartments. Mrs Laurie, Margaret and I were very unwell all the time we were at Paris. Remained in Paris till 24, seeing all that was to be seen. Very

cold. Started 8 o'clock train.
24. Got to Boulogne at 3, dined and slept Hotel *de* Bath.
25. Sailed *at 11*, got over by 1. Had a private room Folkstone, came by rail 10 after 4, got to station 10 before 8, home at 9.
29. (Margaret?) Not recovered from her cold, called in Wade.
November 2. Popery. Marylebone vestry, agreed to second Mr Elliott's motion against papal aggression, to the Queen, but would oppose any memorial to the Bishop of London, said he was the cause of all the michiefs. This appeared in the papers and produced a great noise.
7. Lord John Russel's famous letter to the Bishop of Durham appeared in the 'Times'. At the Common Council this day Mr Blak moved the suspension of the standing orders and then moved a vote of thanks to him for his letter. I supported the committee by a speech, greatly applauded. Mr Richard Taylor said I was the first that had attacked traditions and I was by acclamation added to the committee.
8. Went with the deputation to Lord John who was delighted. I went to the Lord Mayor's swearing in, gave notice I would move an address to the Queen next Court of Aldermen.
9. Peter Northall Laurie made a great speech at Marylebone vestry against P. and P[145]. In the evening dined with the Lord Mayor and in returning thanks for the aldermen made a speech which made a great sensation. Told the ministers if they did not take the lead we would, which was quoted by Barratt all papers.
19. Court of Aldermen moved an address to the Queen written as usual by Peter, seconded by Farebrother, unanimous.
25. Great meeting Guildhall of merchants. Peter found there was nothing about Puseyism, he asked the committee to added a clause, they refused, and proposed it to the great meeting, carried by acclamation. A great victory.
December 10. Went to Windsor with address, see particulars in Letts. Kissed the Queen's hand. Never did so large a number of aldermen and commoners go up with an address. Dined at home, had chariot *and horses* at Slough paid expences by the City, a very dark damp day.
20. Peter Northall Laurie took his seat, Court of Saddlers.
21. Wardmote, no opposition, a vote and resolution against P. and P.
25. Christmas. At Marshall's, came home 22d. Peter Laurie being heir at law to Miss Jack and in the will directed Peter Laurie to take the name of Northall before Laurie in compliment to Lady Laurie and Miss Jack's mother who's maiden name was Northall.

1851.
February 22. Spoke against the non-attendance of aldermen at the Old Bailey and Marylebone vestry. Whitmore motion to lay down more or rather to repair Oxford Street with wood. *I opposed.* An overwhelming majority against him.
25. Carried my motion in the Court of Aldermen that the senior could not be

relieved from duty and that if an aldermen was six months absent they considered his seat vacant. Sir G. Carroll came from Naples to keep his seat.
March 6. Attended levêe.
25. Court of Aldermen, vote of condolence to Lady Pirie proposed by Thompson, seconded by me. Agreed to do away with adjourned *sessions.*
April 21. Easter Monday, took Mr and Mrs Jones, gave tickets to Mr and Mrs Johnston.
29. Court of Aldermen, Thompson declined to remove to Bridge ward, vacant by the death of Sir C. Hunter.
May 1. Opening the Great Exhibition. Seats were reserved for the Lord Mayor and aldermen, who had season tickets. I bought one for Margaret and myself, but afraid of heat I rode about the outside and nothing could be more admirable than the arrangement and the conduct of the people. The Queen with Prince Albert went at 12 in half state.
2. Unwell. The exhibition grand, greatly exceeded my expection.
3. Shewed up fast women and snobs in vestry, in 'Observer'.
June 12. Took the chair for Cunming's testimonial, Freemasons', was elected chairman and treasurer.
30. Peel's statue, Behenes chosen. The Reverend Mr Perring, brother to the late Sir John Perring, whom I never saw, appointed me his executor, but I declined to act.
July 9. Ball at Guildhall to the Queen a failure. Musgrove a baronet, sheriffs knighted. In the morning a meeting of the Union Bank all great applause, 7 per cent.
10. Reversionary meeting to desolve (society). Defeated by great majority.
August 1. Peter and his wife went to Holland by Dover.
19. Andrew, Janet and Alexander came from Edinburgh by Carlisle and reached the station at 1 o'clock. Dined, then drove to Westminster, went to Hampton Court, Windsor, saw all the sights until 29 August, all entered in Lett's dairy.
29. Went to York, Scarborough and after parting with our Edinburgh friends at York 30, remained at Scarbro till 6 September then went to Harrowgate.
9. Peterbro, Harwich, Lowestoft and returned 15 to London.
October 11. Exhibition clossed.
November 6. The Common Council having agreed to get a Bill for the aldermen to be elected every 7 years, I moved this day according to notice to recind the last vote, carried it (for) 79, against 35, majority 44. Greatly delighted at the result.
9. Going through a dense mob, Fore Street, to see the Lord Mayor's procession, was robbed of my valuable watch.
13. Went to Brighton, Bedford a good hotel. Took house, Marine Parade No. 12, at 12 guineas a week. Had 3 horses, all the servants to Brighton, was cold weather all the time.
15. Returned from Brighton.

St Thomas's day. No opposition.
Christmas Day. Dined at home.

1852.
January 18. Mrs Northall Laurie, a boy, afterward named Reginald.
February 10. Having been robbed of my watch as stated above on the 9th November 1851, when the discovery was made of my loss at the Union Bank, Peter at once said, 'Never mind, I will give you one' and this 10 February he gave me a very handsome watch, a repeater, and I believe the best that could be made.
18. This day the friends of the Reverend Dr Cumming met to present to him a testimonial. I was elected treasurer and chairman.
April 1. This day according to promise, I had Margaret Laurie presented to the Queen by her aunt Mrs Northall Laurie. She was 18 years of age, 7 April and I had her presented while I was young enough and able to go with her[146] as a proff of me attachment.
10. Mrs Cox, Margaret and I *and Thomas Turner* went to St Leonards for Easter, where we remained, very comfortable till Tuesday and while there got intimate with Mr W. Brown, Mr and Mrs Brown whom we had met at Mrs Bently's.
21. Allowed Margaret to have presentation ball, which was attended by 100 people asked by her uncle and aunt.
May 8. Dinner to Lord Derby and the ministers. I was very ill from the heat of the gas. Took Margaret with me.
13. Queen's birthday. Mr Northall and Mrs Northall Laurie went with Margaret and I to the drawing room.
15. A cob came down with me, Regent's Park and bruised my foot, but not badly.
June and July. Botanic gardens etc etc.
July 14. Union Bank meeting as before quite satisfactory. I was again reelected chairman or governor.
30. Peter, Fanny, Margaret and I with Thomas started for Germany at ½ past 10 by Dover and Calais, slept St Omer. Went up the Rhine as far as Bale, returned by Paris and got to London 2d September. Particulars in Lett's dairy.
September 24. Margaret not being very well and tired of Mr Wade, Miss Russell and her went to Dr Robert Lee who ordered her to Brighton and to be kept very quiet.
30. Margaret and I and Ann went to Brighton to the Bristol, a very good hotel. 4 horses, coachman and groom came to Brighton on Saturday.
October 12. Took a house, 127 King's Road at 9 guineas a week for a month, a wretchedly furnished house but a good situation. Very bad weather all the time.
November 9. Returned heartily sick of Brighton. Peter and Fanny had a house, Lower Rock Gardens for 6 weeks.
10. Called and told Town Clerk I would not go in the procession or to St Paul's

at the Duke of Wellington's funeral.
12. Saw lying in state at Chelsea Hospital and crowd a mob. *George and John Laurie from New York.*
17. Went and saw St Paul's fitted up.
18. The great Duke's funeral, grand. See the public records. Nothing ever was like it, the behaviour of the people etc.
24. A splendid dinner given to the American minister by W. Brown, M.P. where I met the leading radicals at Fenton's.
December 8. The Lord Mayor('s) dinner 9 November was postponed till after the Duke's funeral and was celebrated at Guildhall, December 6th. Lord Derby and the ministers present. I took Mr W. Brown *with me* and Mrs Brown.
21. Wardmote. Stacy resigned and Ward elected in his stead.
25. Christmas, dined at Johns, Lloyds's and Laurie's. I enjoyed good health all the year except the cold, sprain, and in Germany and Brighton.

1853.
January 3. Mr (and) Mrs Brown having a few days ago asked me to allow Margaret to go with the American minister Mr Ingersoll and his neice Margaret Wilcocks to be a week with them upon a visit, I consented and saw them off at the Euston station. They had a very gay week at Richmon Hill, *Liverpool*, Mr Brown's house, dined at the chief merchants, at Liverpool balls, etc etc. The party returned 11 January.
25. Made Margaret a present of a vote at the India House, cost £2731 5s and transfered and accepted by her this day at the India House.
February 3. Attended the American reception, 45 Portland, very full great *people.*
9. Dined with the Surrey magistrates as Silvester's friend the chairman.
15. Attended Dr Cunming's committee and gave him about (£)1,300 as a testimonial.
March 2. Had Mr Ingersoll at Old Bailey dinner to meet Lord Campbell.
13. Heard Dr Cavedish at the Caledonian, clever but repulsive.
14. Ingersoll's 2d reception.
25. Margaret and I to Dr Cumming, a great preacher, none like him. Peter, Johnson, Smirke and Obbard went to view the estates in Kent. I promised to join them at Ramsgate 26 March, but wrote it was too cold and declined going.
28. Declined to dine this day being Easter Monday, being tired of public *dinners.*
April 1. Return of bronchitis.
9. Address to the Queen, I proposed and John seconded; a boy.
May 14. Margaret went to Richmond with Mrs Brown to remain a week at Richmond, the Castle. Mrs Brown has taken an uncommon fancy to Margaret.
15. Went and lunched with Browns, Richmond, kind people. Chamberlain Brown died.

18. Peabody's great entertainment Star and Garter, Richmond. 140 dined, half English, half American, the American minister, Miss Wilcocks, Mr and Mrs Brown. A concert after dinner, Grise and Maris sang. Got home ¼ to 1.
31. Close of the poll. Key 3179, Scott 2912, majority 267.
June 1. Bay cob came down and sprained my wrist. Peter with me.
4. Address to the Queen. Met the Lord Mayor in state in the Strand. Fell in, palace at 3. I, as mover, kissed the Queen's hand, also alderman as seconder. Home at 4 o'clock.
6. Heard from Coldstream that A. Thomson died on the 3. He left London on 19 May. He was the oldest friend I had in London, for 30 or 40 years he was the constant companion to myself. He was a well informed, well read man and I valued highly, for his honor and integrity I had made him an executor to my will.
7. A Court of Aldermen when I declined going to the Bridge Without, saying I would never leave my friends in Aldersgate ward.
11. Margaret Laurie very ill, confined to bed, sent for Mr Stone.
16. Secured the American minister and niece to dine with the Browns at Holford and had my head broiled under a gas lamp. Made me very, very ill and remained ill till 1 July, when for the first time got upon Beauty which fell after she got of, resolved she should not ride Beauty again. Put Beauty in harness.
July 10. Went to Bridewell sermon, bishop of Landaff. Was so ill that Peter and Margaret were alarmed, sent for Wade, who came 10 at night, gave blue pills etc. Next morning very early put on a blister on my chest and made me remain in bed. Came 3 times. The same on the following day. Took severe medecines to prepare for tomorrow.
16. Bank annual meeting, got out of bed and went but was very ill, took the chair at 12, very nervous, could not speak, came home and went again to bed. Very ill all day and all the week. Saw noone, appetite gone and very ill, pulse very quick.
18. Did very wrong in dining with the Union Bank, Albemarle Street, very ill next day[147]. Wade called and ordered a blue pill etc.
21. Peter and Margaret went to York to meet Alexander who was to take her to *Scotland.* Promised at the end of a month to go and fetch Margaret home by Mr Lakes, Mr Brown etc, but was so weak I could not walk. Margaret gave it up and remained till the 3 September, all alone dining with noone and asking noone, lived the life of a hermit for 6 weeks. Peter and Fanny went to Germany, 28 July.
September 3. Margaret and her father came to London. 7th Margaret and I Bristol Hotel. Andrew went to Saddler's ball, then went to Liverpool.
14. Mr and Mrs Northall Laurie returned from Germany.
17. Went to No. 13, Royal Crescent, Brighton with Margaret, 9 guineas a week with stables. Took 2 maids and all the men and horses.
22. Walked a little about Brighton, but very weak.

29. Came to London for 2 days but did not attend the swearing in of sheriffs or election of Lord Mayor. Peter and Fanny came to Rock Gardens[148].
30. Sent off horses etc to London.
November 2 Returned to London.
9. Did not dine Guildhall.
December 9. My letter upon Corporation in 'Times'.

1854.
January. A very bad frost for several weeks.
22. Took seat 71, M(arylebone) church, All Souls too far to walk.
25. Mrs Jones was so kind as to request Mr Stone not to come again to Margaret.
31. Dr Lee ordered Margaret to Hastings for 2 months.
February 4. Margaret and Miss Pringle went to St Leonards.
6. Common Council, election of aldermen debate, for periodical 33, for life 40.
17. Went with James Gatrell to St Leonards and returned 21.
March 11. Horsley and Cecil went to St Leonards.
23. Duke of Cambridge elected Christ's Hospital 216, Lord Mayor 87. Peter and Fanny went to St Leonards, remained a few days.
April 3. Margaret and Miss Pringle returned from St Leonards.
13. Margaret declined going with Browns to Folkston for the holiday.
17. Declined going to Mansion House, Easter Monday. Gave tickets to Bentley's etc.
20. Margaret and I, Ann and James went to Star and Garter, Richmond.
21. Fanny and Peter came and dined with us.
23. We all returned and dined John Laurie at No.6, very cold[149].
24. Scarf and gloves in mourning of James Holford died 9 April, 67[150].
May 17. Peter and Fanny went to Paris ½ past 4.
30. Peter and Fanny returned from Paris.
June 2. Turnbull Dr, wedding.
6. Margaret went with Mr and Mrs Jones to Mrs Middleton.
9. Went to leveée. Margaret came home from Mrs Middleton.
10. Peter, Fanny, Margaret and I went to Crystal Palace. Came home in a 3d class carriage to dine at Fenton's.
15. Peter, Fanny and Margaret went to Ascot races, see Letts.
29. Election of sheriffs, Muggeridge and Crossley chosen. A grand row, Court of Aldermen, Lord Mayor broke up the court.
July 12. Caught a severe cold 10 June and was very ill, could not walk, in great pain shoulders and arms. Attended bank, 15 per cent. A vote of the court for me to sit for my portrait.
13. Dined with the bank, rheumatism much worse.
19. Dined Greenwich.
23. Called in Dr Bright, gave pills etc, no better, and took Brighton medicine till 11 August then went to Tunbridge Wells and very ill there, in great pain.

Went to St Leonards, 14 August, and was well shampood, drove to Hastings.
August 18. Called in Dr Gardiner, clever, likes a fee every 2d visit.
28. Left Hastings and got to Folkstone 8.30, 40 miles, bad road. Appartments at Pavilion, remained at Folkstone till 26 September. *Often with Baldocks, Thins, etc.* Came to town at 3.30. Peter went with us to the Star and Garter where we remained till 9 October.
October 23. Began to sit to Grant for portrait and sat to him 17 times.
November 16. Margaret and Peter went to York. Met her brother and they slept at York and went to Edinburgh 17.
December 20. Herring went to York and came home with Margaret 21.

1855.
January 1. My rheumatism daily better, could now tye my own neckcloth. Dined a little out and was myself again.
18. Margaret with her maid went to Rugby. Mr Baldock met her at Rugby and gave her a cordial reception at their hunting lodge. Very cold. Margaret very happy and pleased with her trip, made an impression on Mr Kenyon who offered her a Spanish mantilla, which I advised her not to accept and gave her one instead.
30. She returned on 30. Thames frozen over.
April 5. Went with Margaret, James and Elizabeth to Cheltenham and to Malvern. Returned April 10th.
16. The Emperor and Empress of the French came and drove through Hyde Park to the Paddington station for Windsor. Emperor and Empress at Guildhall splendidly fitted up, the address read and reply, all the aldermen presentd to the Emperor, he said he knew me very well. I dined with the princes at Mansion House, very stupid, Lord Mayor a bad chairman. See Letts. Emperor and Empress left London for Paris.
27. Davidson and Gordon, Guildhall. This case took me about 17 times, all the newspaper reports were cut and kept as a memorandum to be used if necessary. I appointed the City Solicitor to prosecute but he threw all difficulty in the (way) and at last had the impudence to ask me to get another alderman to sit instead of me which was the second time I was asked. Such a compleament to my skill. They were found guilty and all in prison.

Went to Clifton with Margaret Laurie and Mrs Cox and maid. All the movements in Lett's diary, May 25.
August 9. Went to Star and Garter, returned 19.
20. Went to Liverpool, Mrs Brown's, for 10 days, then to Holyhead, returned by Aberswith and Malvern. 7 September to London. Margaret went to Scotland 21 September and returned 28 November, 9 weeks. An interesting Jews case, 16 October, see Letts.
December 4. The King of Sardinia entertained, Guildhall. My fine boy Cecil died 18 December 1855, and was burried 22 December 1855[151].

1856.

January 2. Went to Sir G. Grey's with the Lord Mayor and deputation from the City upon the reform.

February 5. Paid Hooper for a brougham £80.

9. Mr Bell having been advised to remove the Waterloo from the Wellington statue entrusted to him presented a report to omit Waterloo and substitute the solders' return. I opposed the alteration and we came to a vote, 9 for the change, 13 against. This was a great victory against the officers and others, names in Letts.

15. Mrs Northall a daughter, Rosalind.

March 3. Margaret and Elizabeth went to Baldock's and returned from Huskind's, Bosworth 13, away 10 days.

April 14. Margaret and Elizabeth went to Bournemouth and returned 21 April.

21. Accident riding my cob home after a pleasant ride, opposite No. 12 he fell down on his side after a struggle on his knees, my left leg under him and bruised, painful, resolved not to ride him again.

22. Margaret returned from Bournmouth and went to Lady Belcher at ½ past 4 morning and went with Lady Belcher to Portsmouth, saw the naval review and got home at 12 at night, sent carriage home with Lady Belcher. This trip made Margaret very ill.

29. Proclamation of peace.

May 4. Took possession of No. 60 pew immediately left by Oxonham.

21. Peter Northall Laurie went to France.

29. The Hyde Park illuminations at 11, went after dinner, home ¼ before 1.

June 23. Margaret and Elizabeth went to Bushey and returned 29 July.

August 1. Margaret and Elizabeth went to Liverpool, returned 18. All No. 6 went to Shenley.

7. I went to Shenley, returned 12 August.

September 4. Went to Calais.

5. Slept at Amiens and all the procedings entered in Letts *diary* till the 22 when we returned to London.

October 1. Peter and Fanny went to Dover, Calais etc and returned 15 October.

16. Margaret went for a few days with Louis Huth to Reigate.

November 2. *Dined with Finnis inaguration dinner. Very grand, no gas, London Tavern.*

6. Margaret, Isabel and I went to the Bedford, Brighton and returned 11.

13. Redpath found out.

26. Wrote to the Corporation for Chambers and secured his election for Common Sergeant.

1857.

January 29. Common Council. Lock 48, Bodkin 58, Riddell 77, Chambers 91; 2d poll Chambers 102, Riddell 89.

February 16. Margaret and Mrs Cox went to Hastings and on the 26 went from Hastings to Brighton, 73 Marine Parade.
27. I went to Brighton, returned March 1 to London.
March 7. Margaret and Mrs Cox returned from Brighton.
May 7. Margaret and I went to the Star and Garter, Richmond.
11. Returned from Richmond.
June 22. Lord Campbell's letter.
July 13. Freedom of the City, Frederick of Prussia.
15. Dined and slept Star and Garter after Bank meeting.
23. Mary's wedding, see Letts.
August 12. Mrs Laurie and Margaret went to Lady Carroll's. Margaret and I returned 16th.
27. Shivey went to Bangor with chair and crutches.

M. Scrutton, myself and Mr Capper went to Dover, Lord Warden. Left the Lord Warden, Dover, went to Folkestone September 1 and left for London September 7, left the Scrimgeours at Folkestone.

11. Mr Alderman Rose, Guildhall. Margaret and Miss More met at Manchester, Wednesday, the art treasures, at Mr Sewell's till Saturday 19th.
30. This day met at the Union Bank Scrimgeour, Robert Peter Laurie, Dobbin's clerk, Weston's solicitor, Mr Roll. After Scrimgeour read all the deeds respecting Weston's and Robert Peter Laurie's partnership, the deeds were signed. Weston (£)10,000, Robert Peter Laurie (£)10,000 including (£)5,000 from me lent to Robert and (£)5,000 of his own making 20,000. The firm to be Weston and Laurie, Bill brokers, commencing 1 October 1857 for 3 years. Miss Pringle came for a week on a visit. Peter Northall Laurie broke his leg, laid up at Bangor, *18 August* King George Hotel and did not return till 12 October. Could not stand, a dreadful accident.
October 3. Miss Pringle upon a visit here for week
7. Fast day, a shocking bad sermon, Mr Chaffer.
12. Northall and Mrs Laurie and Beatrice returned from Bangor. Margaret at Moore's Putney Heath and returned 19, Monday.
26. Scotch deputation dined Grillion's.
November 10. Went to the York, Brighton, good rooms.
17. Carried Finnis vote of thanks.
20. A great party, Silvester's, Brighton.
23. Glennie's dinner.
30. Returned from Brighton, no more to the York.
December 3. Queen opened Parliament.
8. Dined with the Saddlers. A dangerous fog.
10. Northall, Fanny and Beatrice, Folkstone, till Monday.
21. Common Council, Aldersgate, no change in members.
25. Dined No. 6, only 4.

1858.

January 1. A large party at[152] John Laurie's, Hyde Park Place.
5. Margaret went to Garner's seasonal party.
8. At home all day, slipped out of bed, bad cold.
10. Very ill, slipped out of bed again.
12. In bed all day. In bedroom till the 19 January.
20. Not well enough to take the chair at the Union Bank.
25. Margaret had cards for Princess Royal's marriage from Bread Street.
30. Margaret went with Lady Chantry to drawing room.

February 5. Capper slept in his own room and I dressed in my dressing room first time since 7 January. Quite well.

March 4. Mr and Mrs Northall Laurie with their children went to Norwood.
20. Went to congratulate Sir George Pollock on reappointment.
30. A vote upon the death of Farebrother.

April 1. Went to Star and Garter, Richmond till 6th. Northall and Fanny Laurie dined Richmond 5 April.
23. Margaret went without her maid to Miss Pringle's till 26.

May 9. Went to hear Guthrie, all the great Scotchmen lords there.
13. Northall Laurie went to Paris and returned 22.
25. Margaret went with Scrutton to Miss Pringle's.

June 7. Star and Garter, John and George Laurie dinner, we remained all night.
21. Sent to Mr Newton for Margaret.
30. Declined to dine at Bridewell dinner.

July 2. House of Commons.
6. Dined Blackwall.
14. North British, Star and Garter.
20. Dischar(g)ed Capper.

August 7. Dr Burrows called, declined Newton at present.
26. William Perkins came to his new place.
30. Last day at the India House.

September 2. Found balance of Peel's statue (£)356 in the name of myself, Masterman and Wire.
3. Miss Pringle and Margaret went to Margate.
13. Went to Tunbridge Wells for a day or two.
21. Margaret and Miss Pringle came from Margate by rail.

October 4. Margaret and Ann went to Chester and then to Brown's, Liverpool, 9th October to meet Brougham, John Roper. Northall Laurie and childern to Folkstone. Wissell removed from Bank.

November 10. Went to Brighton, 2 Queensbury House, 14 guineas, a good house. Took carriage and 3 horses.
19. A fox hunt in brougham.
20. Miss Lyal[153] for a week. Northall, Margaret often at Queensbury Place.

December 8. Returned to London. All now in Letts till the 31 December.

1859.

January 12. Wednesday took chair Union Bank, unanimous.

17. Saunders took model of lower gum, very painful.

27. Teeth put in and fitted well.

31. William Hays came as groom, 16 guineas.

APPENDIX 1

1831.
Sir Peter Laurie's exertions to promote the Conservative club.
A plan *or plot* to keep in Sir John Key in the civic chair for another *year* and to keep out Peter Laurie because he had not joined in the mad enthusiasm in passing the Reform Bill. My friends met at the London Tavern on the 20 September, *Lord Brougham* sent his private secretary to hear my sentiments *at the meeting* and as I could not as an honest man join the cry of the radicals, on the 29 September they started Key against me and after the first seven, 7, days or end of the poll, the numbers were Key 3258, Thorpe 3081, Laurie 2713. The Court of Aldermen returned Thorpe. He declined as was arranged and they put up Key and Thompson.
A 2nd election. That election lasted 7 days when the Court of Aldermen returned Thompson who, as was arranged, declined also. A third election, when at last the Court of Aldermen on the 4th November returned Key and gave up the contest. Thus was I harrassed from 29 September to 4 November at an expence above £1000.

1832.
Having secured at a considerable expense the watermen liverymen I filled the Common Hall and was elected Mayor without opposition. Stated at my Lord Mayor's dinner 9th November that during my year of office the Mansion House should be neutral ground marking a contrast between Key's year and mine[154] and I invited Duke of Wellington, Peel, Gouldbaum, Mr Salisbury etc but such was the fear of a friendly reception during the reform mania that they declined on the morning of the 9th November.

Always promoting the cause of the Conservatives, I was determined to have the leaders of the party at the Mansion House and wrote to the Marquis of Salisbury who secured for me Peel *and 12 leading Conservatives. Peel* I made the hero of the evening and gave him and the Privy councillors etc etc. The 'Times' on the following day accused me of packing the meeting with tories and Hume in the House of Commons also mentioned the reception of Peel as a toast. This gave great courage to the Conservatives in the City.

Queen Adelaide having agreed to attend at the anniversary of the childern going to St Paul's I invited her to the Mansion House which she condescendingly accepted. My object was to remove the reports that she was unpopular, and having met her at Temple Bar and to St Paul's and afterwards to the Mansion House and upon her return the populace were *everywhere* enthusiastic in their applause. James Brougham mentioned to me that the offence I gave to the government by thus making the people rally round the Queen, would never be forgiven, and what increased their rage was the conservative vote of thanks given to me by the Court of Aldermen for entertaining and entroducing them all at the Mansion House to the Queen etc. I was censured by Pearson and some of the members of the Common Council. This enabled me to lay before the *Court* the particulars of the Queen's visit and was printed by and recorded by the Corporation. This was my first victory over the radicals.

Notwithstanding all my efforts to aid my party I got an unanimous vote of thanks on the 29 September in Common Hall. The newspapers all applauded me, the 'Standard' said after other remarks, 'This is the conservative style of earning popularity, for conservative, we are proud to say, Sir Peter is.' Every paper praised me in their leading article but the 'Times'. The 'Times' however, made ample amends in 1835 when that paper became Conservative.

1834.

December 6. The Duke of Buccleuch wrote that he and his friends had started me for the Haddington Burghs. On the 11 I wrote and declined, but on the 17 I received a letter from Sir F. Drumond saying he had employed agents in the 5 Burghs. I immediately sent my nephew Peter Laurie who found at Dunbar and Haddington that I was too late and he gave up the contest after spending about £200, causing Steuart to spend money also.

1835.

Went to hustings and made a strong Conservative speech for Captain Wood, which was greatly praised and did much good. I now determined to go on in my endevors to make the Common Council Conservative. On the 18 March I made a *Conservative* speech against periodical elections *of aldermen* which was much liked although the question was carried against me. I published my speech greatly emproved by my nephew and it produced a good effect.

Having been a steward to Peel's great dinner at Merchant Tailors' I was one of a deputation to ask Sir Robert to allow us to give him a dinner in Marlebone, which he declined. Got up the speech, and answer, and published it (sic) in newspapers.

During 1836 *and 1837* attended regularly the Common Council, they becoming more conservative. The first proof *I had was that* Mr Wilson presented a letter from Mr Pearson to the Duchess of Kent when we went up with an address upon her daughter attaining 18 years of age, got a vote of censure against Wilson although supported by the radicals. *At the committee for conducting the*

Queen's visit to the City, I attended daily and got many many invitations for my party and every day I saw a political change taking place. The reception of the Duke of Wellington and Sir Robert Peel proved I was right.
November 16. In a correspondence published in the 'Post' and an interview with the Lord Chancellor, after seeing Lords Abingdon and Wharncliffe I succeeded in preventing 15 radical magistrates being appointed for Marlebone.

1838.
The first decisive demonstration of the Conservative power was when Sir M. Wood proposed to give a dinner (to) the ambassadors who came to the coronation. I asked who were to be invited to meet them, he said none but the ministers. I moved tha(t) 15 of each side of the Lords and 25 each side of the Commons be invited. I carried my motion and in the committee I named the 15 Lords and 25 Commoners, and Sir M. Wood 15 Lords and 25 Commoners, nothing could be more fair. I then knew my strength, got Sir F. Burdett whom the radicals most hated, invited. Another proof I had; the Common Council by a majority *had* voted that the aldermen should be elected periodically, now voted by a large majority to be for life and all the radical votes respecting the reform of the Corporation were recinded.

1839.
When Sir M. Wood got his friends together with the intention of addressing the Queen to thank her for recalling[155] Lord Melborne and the ministers who had *now* returned to office, 6 of us called our friends in the Corporation together and I called over the names. 107 were declared against any such address. We summoned them, 80 came, we were then certain and when the discussion took place I got Anderton to propose the previous question, I seconded in and the numbers for the address 75, for *the* previous question 121, giving the Conservatives a majority of 46, thus proving that the great Corporation chiefly discovered by the management and skill of Peter Laurie, Lambett, Jones and others, and had a great opportunity *like this* not thus occurred we might have gone on, the Conservatives not knowing their own strength and numbers and never dreaming of making the attempt.

FOOTNOTES

1. Wreath: a bank or drift of snow (Scottish, c1725 ff).
2. 'only' deleted.
3. ? Mertoun, South West Berwickshire.
4. 'Edinburgh 1793' marginated.
5. A tragedy by John Home, the main character of which is Young Norval.
6. 'thought I was' interlined to replace 'who was'.
7. Interlined to replace 'they'.
8. Interlined to replace 'from'.
9. 'London difficulty in getting work' marginated.
10. Spouting Clubs (or societies): met to practice recitation and oratory.
11. '1797' marginated.
12. A play by George Colman Junior, which includes characters named Mortimer and Wilford.
13. '1798' marginated.
14. A play translated from the German by Mrs Elizabeth Inchbald. It was this play which was to be performed by the characters in *Mansfield Park* (Jane Austen). Frederick is an important character.
15. Perhaps taken from Oliver Goldsmith's play of the same name.
16. '1799' marginated.
17. 'Richards heir to the lease of Sandersdean' marginated.
18. 'to be given' interlined to replace 'for'.
19. 'Sobriety' marginated.
20. A play by Thomas Morton, which includes a character named Walter.
21. 'kept my' interlined to replace 'completed'.
22. 'took' deleted.
23. 'terms' interlined to replace 'than'.
24. 'Religion' marginated.
25. 'A love scrape Paull' marginated.
26. 'Miss Bunyan' marginated.
27. The Great Review of the Volunteers by George III took place in Hyde Park in 1799.
28. 'Engaged to go to the York company' marginated.
29. 1776–1850; and authoress whose most famous book was *The Scottish Chiefs or the Life of Sir William Wallace.*
30. 'Refused to go to York' marginated.
31. 'Began business' marginated.
32. 'Reflection on the drama and its temptations' marginated.
33. 'Pushing business' marginated.
34. 'Looking out for a wife' marginated.
35. 'Pushing business to great success' marginated.
36. 'Miss Jack' marginated.
37. 'Miss Jack bold interview' marginated.

38. 'Hans Place' marginated.
39. 'Mrs Trotter, first meeting' marginated.
40. 'Generous Mr Jack' marginated.
41. 'Greenwich' marginated.
42. 'Supplying belts good hit in business' marginated.
43. 'John came up' marginated.
44. 'First East India contract' marginated.
45. 'Generous and just conduct of Mr R. Birnie' marginated.
46. 'Took a fancy to Peter' marginated.
47. 'a few' interlined to replace '11'.
48. 'Robert Peter came to London' marginated.
49. 'I hope' deleted.
50. 'My great contract' marginated.
51. 'Maberley conduct' marginated.
52. 'Last the East India Contracts' marginated.
53. '1815+6' marginated.
54. 'Helensburgh, Dumbartonshire' marginated.
55. 'Turnham Green' marginated.
56. 'Water companies monoply' marginated.
57. 'Queen's trial' marginated.
58. 'Highlands' marginated.
59. 'Dined with Lord Mayor 1st time' marginated.
60. 'had' deleted.
61. 'Lord Mayor' interlined to replace 'magistrates'.
62. 'Altered the mode of hanging at Newgate' marginated.
63. '11 Feb 1824 paid Sir George Naylor £54 12(s) for registering the name of Laurie instead of Snaddon' marginated.
64. 'occasion' interlined to replace 'reason'.
65. 'Bubble companies' marginated.
66. 'A tour to Cheltenham, Plymouth' marginated.
67. 'promised I should be in the first' deleted.
68. 'alderman' interlined to replace 'magistrate'.
69. 'in Cornwall Terrace' interlined to replace 'or rather sold the terrace'.
70. 'Went into the ward Aldersgate' marginated.
71. 'My address' marginated.
72. 'Sworn in' marginated.
73. 'The appointment of Deputy Lieutenant was gazetted but I have forgotten the date' marginated.
74. 'Opening court Middlesex' marginated.
75. 'Went to Switzerland, up the Rhine' marginated.
76. A paragraph, repeating the information about the lunatic asylum and opening the county court, has been deleted here – as it was by Sir Peter.
77. '31 January 1828 Was summoned as a juryman, took the City lists and charter to show I was excused as an alderman. Mr Justice Bayley said I might go to any other engagement I had' marginated.
78. 'Peter upon the Livery' marginated.
79. 'court' interlined to replace 'Livery'.
80. 'Omitted at the proper date' marginated.
81. '29 September 1830' marginated.
82. 'Michaelmas day' marginated.
83. 'Mansion' interlined to replace 'Guildha'.

84. 'said he would not support the reform' interlined to replace 'Venables elected instead of Ward'.
85. 'Election' marginated.
86. '2nd election' marginated.
87. '3rd election' marginated.
88. 'new' deleted.
89. 'request the King to sit for his po' deleted.
90. 'Tour to the Isle of Wight' marginated.
91. '28' marginated.
92. '1st sitting Mansion House' marginated.
93. 'all' repeated.
94. 'ballot' interlined to replace 'poll'.
95. 'Marlebone dinner' marginated.
96. 'Marlebone ball' marginated.
97. 'March 16' marginated.
98. 'Very ill' marginated.
99. 'Vote of thanks for entertaining the Queen' marginated.
100. 'A charge against me by Common Council for entertaining the Queen' marginated.
101. 'published' interlined to replace 'printed'.
102. 'Melvile's sermon, St Ann's' marginated.
103. The following entries were deleted.

24. Lady Laurie and Miss Wilkie went to Tunbridge Wells and intended to be out 6 weeks, the chariot and pair greys and coachman. Same day given my conservancy dinner at Greenwich.

30. Anderton's party, dined at Blackwall, 40 dined chiefly radicals.

104. Changed from 'towed up'.
105. Altered from 'completed'.
106. 'Dinner given to medical officers' marginated.
107. 'Common Hall' marginated.
108. 'About 50 of' deleted.
109. 'Lord Mayor's Day' marginated.
110. 'Cope elected governor of Newgate' added at foot of page.
111. 'my' deleted.
112. 'answer' interlined to replace 'address'.
113. ie a knee-length portrait, usually showing the subject seated.
114. 'with' deleted.
115. 'The Carleton Club sent for me. Saw Lord G. Somerset who advised me to start for Nottingham and said it would cost (£)2000. Declined' maginated.
116. 'quixotic' deleted.
117. 'a vote of thanks to' interlined to replace 'the health of'.
118. 'presented' interlined to replace 'gave'.
119. 'This is a great error.... 1849.' added in pencil. The revised comment appears to have been made by Sir Peter.
120. 'the' deleted.
121. 'I' interlined to replace 'but'.
122. Tasmania. Alexander Reid was Sir Peter's grand-nephew.
123. '95 to 64' interlined to replace '77 to 53'.
124. 'at' interlined to replace 'for'.
125. Altered from 'male'.
126. 'Puzzites' interlined to replace 'Peuzyities'; he means Puseyites (ie the High Church followers of Edmund Pusey and the Oxford Movement).

127. 'Stockdale and Hansard' marginated.
128. James Harmer was possibly the last aldermanic candidate not to be elected Lord Mayor (until the advent of women aldermen). In fact he came bottom of the poll in 1840. Although claimed as a friend by Sir Peter, he was the proprietor of the 'Weekly Despatch' described as a 'blackguard newspaper', and was also a free thinker.
129. 'General Election' marginated.
130. 'ballot' deleted.
131. 'Hollond' marginated.
132. Altered from '58'.
133. 'as' deleted.
134. 'Caoutchouc Company, vote of thanks from Samuel Mosley and others framed and glazed in dining room' marginated.
135. 'are' interlined to replace 'were'.
136. 'hired' interlined to replace 'got'.
137. This entry (12 May) is struck through and marginated 'Copied from 1843 instead of 1844'.
138. 'Dickens's (The) Chimes' marginated.
139. 'gave up to' interlined to replace 'left for'.
140. 'Reformed the Common Council, no more locking in' marginated.
141. 'join Lady Laurie at' deleted.
142. 'some' interlined to replace 'we'.
143. At head of page.
144. 'committee' deleted.
145. 'P and P': presumably Popery and Puseyism.
146. 'Margaret presented at Court' marginated.
147. 'Capel' deleted.
148. 'New Strand' deleted.
149. 'Margaret went alone to Dr Lee who said she was well' marginated.
150. 'Called in Mr Longinde' marginated.
151. This is the only reference to this person and raises many questions; none answerable from Sir Peter's Journal.
152. 'home' deleted.
153. Spelt 'Llyall'; second 'l' deleted.
154. 'should be neutral....Key's year and mine' deleted.
155. 'thank her for recalling' interlined to replace 'recall'.

Appendix 2

Brief details of Aldermen, Common Councillors, M.P.s, Saddlers, and others mentioned in the Journal.

Abbreviations used:

A: Alderman of the City of London
CC: Common Councilman of the City of London
Co.:Livery Company
M: Lord Mayor of London
S: Sheriff of London and Middlesex

Anderton, James: CC Farringdon Without 1836-66.
03Ansley, John: merchant taylor; A Bread Street 1800-35, Bridge Without 1835; S 1805-6; M 1807-8.

Birnie, Sir Richard: a saddler with Macintosh and Co., Haymarket; later magistrate at Bow Street and a J.P.
Brown, Anthony: fishmonger; CC Billingsgate 1803-21; A Billingsgate 1821-44; S 1824-5; M 1826-7; City chamberlain 1844-53.
Bruce, James: a saddler who had a shop opposite Tiviot Row, Bristo, Edinburgh c1792, to whom Sir Peter was apprenticed.
Byng, George: M.P. Middlesex 1835, 1837.

Capper, John H.: clerk for criminal business at the Home Office, 1824.
Carroll, Sir George: spectaclemaker; A Candlewick 1839-60, S 1837-8, M 1846-7, president St Bartholemew's Hospital 1854-60.
Challis, Thomas: butcher, A Cripplegate 1843-74; S 1846-7; M 1852-3; M.P. Finsbury 1852-7; master Butchers' Co. 1839-40.
Cole, Thomas: treasurer Bridewell and Bethlehem Hospitals 1831-5.
Copeland, William Taylor: goldsmith; A Bishopsgate 1829-68; S 1828-9; M 1835-6; M.P. Coleraine 1831, Stoke on Trent 1837, 1857, prime warden Goldsmiths' Co. 1837-8; president Bridewell and Bethlehem Hospitals 1861-8; treasurer Sons of the Clergy 1841-68.
Cowan, Sir John; wax chandler; CC Broad Street 1817-31; A Broad Street 1831-42; S 1831-2; M 1837-8; master Wax Chandlers' Co. 1836-8.
Cox, Robert Albion: goldsmith; CC Aldersgate 1794-1800; A Aldersgate 1813-26; S 1801-2; prime warden Goldsmiths' Co, 1818-19.
Crawford, William: M.P. City of London 1833.
Crowder, John: playing card maker; CC Farringdon Within 1800-23, deputy

1814; A Farringdon Within 1823-30; S 1825-6; M 1829-30; master Stationers' Co, 1829-30.

Curtis, Sir William: draper; A Tower 1785-1821, Bridge Without 1821-9; S 1788-9; M 1795-6; M.P. City of London 1790, 1796, 1802, 1806, 1807, 1812, Blechingly 1820.

Denman, Sir Thomas: common sergeant for City 1823, attorney general 1830; lord chief justice for England 1832.

Dixon, Samuel: fishmonger; CC Tower 1786-1837; awarded plate by Sir Peter Laurie in 1833.

Duke, Sir James: spectaclemaker; CC Billingsgate 1831-40; A Farringdon Without 1840-73; S 1836-7; M 1848-9; master Spectaclemakers' Co. 1840-1, 1847-8, 1849-50, 1860-1; Salters' Co. 1853-4; Loriners' Co. 1855-6; M.P. Boston 1837, 1841, 1847, City of London 1849, 1852, 1857, 1859.

Eagleton, Edward: haberdasher; CC Farringdon Within 1821-7, 1830-55, deputy 1847; A Farringdon Within 1855-7; master Haberdashers' Co. 1851.

Evans, William: S 1839-40.

Farebrother, Charles: vinter; A Lime Street 1826-58; S 1826-7; M 1833-4; masters Vinters' Co. 1835,1852, 1856; contested Lambeth 1835.

Finnis, Thomas Quested: bowyer; CC Tower 1833-48, deputy 1838; A Tower 1848-83; S 1848-9; M 1856-7; masters Bowyers' Co. 1856-8; treasurer Sons of the Clergy 1874-82.

Flowers, Sir Charles: framework knitter; A Cornhill 1801-34; S 1799-1800; M 1808-9; master Framework Knitters' Co. 1801-2; treasurer London Hospital 1812-14.

Freshfield, James William: solicitor to Bank of England; M.P. Penryn 1835-41, 1852-7, Boston 1851-2.

Garratt, John: goldsmith; CC Bridge 1810-11; A Bridge 1821-32; S 1821-2; M 1824-5; contested Lambeth 1826.

Gibbs, Michael: fishmonger; CC Walbrook 1818-38, deputy 1832; A Walbrook 1838-51; S 1840-1; M 1844-5.

Gibson and Son: army saddlers at 9 Coventry Street, London c.1796-7.

Glyn, Sir Richard Carr: salter; A Bishopsgate 1790-1829 Bridge Without 1829-35; S 1790-1; M 1798-9; president Bridewell and Bethlehem Hospitals 1798-1833.

Godsman: a saddler in St Martin's Street, London c.1796.

Goulburn, the Right Honourable Henry: M.P. Cambridge University 1833.

Hall, Benjamin: M.P. Marylebone 1837.

Harmer, James: spectaclemaker; CC Farringdon Without 1825-33; A Farringdon Without 1833-40; S 1833-4; master Spectaclemakers' Co. 1831-2, 1843-4.
Harvey, Daniel Whittle: girdler; CC Bishopsgate 1814-19; contested election for A Portsoken 1831; M.P. Colchester 1818, 1820, 1826, 1830, 1832, 1837; Commissioner of City Police.
Hastings, Warren: governor-general of India impeached for supposed misconduct in administration in 1787.
Herries, the Right Honourable John C.; M.P. Harwich 1833.
Heygate, Sir William: merchant taylor; CC Cripplegate Within 1809-12; A Coleman Street 1812-43; S 1811-12; M 1822-3; M.P. Sudbury 1818-26; City chamberlain 1834-4.
Hooper, John Kinnersley: vinter; CC Queenhithe 1831-40, deputy 1835; A Queenhithe 1840-54; S 1842-3; M 1847-8; master Vinters' Co. 1849; president St Bartholemew's Hospital 1848-54.
Horne, Sir William: M.P. Newton, Isle of Wight 1833; solicitor general.
Hudson, Thomas: receiver Bridewell and Bethlehem Hospitals 1835.
Hughes, William Hughes: cordwainer; A Portsoken 1832-3, Bread Street 1843-8; master Cordwainers' Co. 1843-4; M.P. Oxford 1830, 1833; sheriff Hampshire 1843.
Hume, Joseph: M.P. Aberdeen 1826, Middlesex 1835, Kilkenny 1837.
Humphery, John: tallow chandler; A Aldgate 1835-63; S 1832-3; M 1842-3; master Tallow Chandlers' Co. 1838-9 1858-9; M.P. Southwark 1832-52; candidate Chamberlain 1844.
Hunter, Sir Claudius Stephen: merchant taylor; A Bassishaw 1804-34, Bridge Without 1835-51; S 1808-9; M 1811-12.
Hunter, William: upholder; CC Coleman Sreet 1825-43; A Coleman Street 1843-56; S 1844-5; M 1851-2; master Upholders' Co. 1845-6.

Illidge, John: S 1834-5.

Johnson, John: spectaclemaker; A Dowgate 1839-48; S 1836-7; M 1845-6; master Spectaclemakers' Co. 1833-4, 1837-40; contested Plymouth 1841, City of London 1847.
Johnson, John Edward: treasurer Bridewell and Bethlehem Hospitals 1848-68, president 1868.
Johnson, Thomas: cooper; A Portsoken 1833-44; S 1838-9; M 1840-1.

Kelly, Thomas: plaisterer; CC Farringdon Within 1823-30; A Farringdon Within 1830-55; S 1825-6; M 1836-7; master Plaisterers' Co. 1831-2.
Key, Sir John: stationer; A Langbourne 1823-51, Bridge Without 1851-3; S 1824-5; M 1830-2; master Stationers' Co. 1830-3; city chamberlain 1853-8;

M.P. City of London 1832.

Lainson, John: spectaclemaker; A Bread Street 1835-43; S 1835-6.
Laurie, John; S 1845-6; M.P. Barnstaple 1857-9.
Laurie, Sir Peter: saddler; saddler and harnessmaker at 293, then 296 Oxford Street; A Aldersgate 1826-61; S 1823-4; M 1832-3; master Saddlers' Co. 1833-4; president Bridewell and Bethlehem Hospitals 1833-61; J.P. Middlesex and Westminster 1825; deputy lieutenant Middlesex 1826; vestryman in Marylebone 1825-32, 1843-61; trustee of the roads Marylebone 1825; governor of Union Bank London 1829-61.
Laurie, Peter Northall: common pleader 1842.
Law, the Honourable Charles Ewan: common sergeant 1830-3; recorder 1833-50; M.P. Cambridge University 1835.
Lawrence, William: carpenter; CC Bread Street 1832-48; A Bread Street 1848-55; S 1849-50; master Carpenters' Co. 1848-9.
Legg, Moses Edward: needlemaker; CC Bread Street 1824-34.
Lorkin, John: brewer; CC Aldersgate Without 1816-65, deputy 1833, 1837.
Lucas, Matthew Prime: vintner; CC Tower 1797-1821; A Tower 1821-48; S 1822-3; M 1827-8; masters Vinters' Co. 1838; president St Bartholemew's Hospital 1831-48.
Lyall, George, broderer; M.P. City of London 1833, 1841; director East India Company 1830-51.

Magnay, Sir William: stationer; A Vintry 1838-57; S 1841-2; M 1843-4; master Stationers' Co. 1847-8.
Mahon, the Honourable Philip Henry: M.P. Wooton Basset 1831.
Marshall, Sir Chapman: innholder; CC Vintry 1817-32; A Bridge 1832-59; S 1830-1; M 1839-40; master Innholders' Co. 1835-6.
Masterman, John: M.P. City of London 1847, 1852; director East India Company 1823-54.
Matthews, William: innholder; CC Aldersgate Within 1833.
Maule, the Honourable Fox: under secretary of State at Home Office 1837.
Maxton, Joshua: a saddler in High Street, Edinburgh c1793,
Maxton, Joseph: a saddler at 20 North Bridge, Edinburgh c1800.
Mirehouse, John: common pleader; common sergeant 1833-50.
Moon, Sir Francis Graham: stationer; CC Broad Street 1831-44; A Portsoken 1844-71, Bridge Without 1871; M 1854-5; masters Loriners' Co. 1854-5, Stationers' Co. 1855-6.
Muggeridge, Sir Henry: innholder; CC Castle Baynard 1843-53; A Castle Baynard 1853-62; S 1854-5; master Innholders' Co. 1863-4.
Murray, Sir George; general, chairman Scots School Society.
Musgrove, Sir John: clothworker; CC Broad Street 1835-42; A Broad Street

1842-72; S 1843-4; M 1850-1; master Clothworkers' Co. 1843, 1862; president St Thomas' Hospital 1851-81.

Pearson, Charles: M.P. Lambeth 1850; City solicitor 1840-62.
Peck, Robert: S 1832-3.
Peto, Samuel Morton: elected S 1849 but did not accept office; M.P. Norwich 1847, 1852.
Pilcher, Jeremiah: S 1842-3; contested Southwark 1845.
Pirie, Sir John: plaisterer; A Cornhill 1834-51; S 1831-2; M 1841-2: master Plaisterers' Co. 1828-9; president St Thomas' Hospital 1842-51; candidate for chamberlain 1843.
Poland, Sir William Henry: S 1830-1.
Pollock, David: saddler; saddler to the King, last master of Sir Peter Laurie; shops in Piccadilly and Charing Cross.
Portman, Edward Berkeley: M.P. Dorsetshire 1831-3; Marylebone 1833.
Poynder, John: clerk and solicitor Bridewell and Bethlehem Hospitals 1805-45; also a theological writer and evangelical worker with missionary societies.
Price, Ralph: treasurer Bridewell 1836-48.

Raphael, Alexander: S 1834-5; contested Evesham 1830, Pontefract 1835; M.P. Carlow County 1835.
Roe, Sir Frederick Adair: chief magistrate Bow Street, central criminal court 1834.
Rose, Sir William Anderson: Spectaclemaker; CC Queenhithe 1849-54; A Queenhithe 1854-81; S 1855-6; M 1862-3; master Spectaclemakers' Co. 1857-8, 1877-8, Loriners' Co. 1866-7; Wax Chandlers' Co. 1872-4; M.P. Southampton 1862-5.
Solomons, Sir David: cooper; A Aldgate 1835, Portsoken 1844, Cordwainer 1846-73; S 1835-6; M 1855-6; master Coopers' Co. 1841-2; M.P. Greenwich 1851, 1859-73; sheriff Kent 1839-40; refused to take oath for A as a Jew in 1835 and 1844.
Scales, Michael: CC Portsoken 1829-31; candidate for S 1831; contested Portsoken as A 1831, 1833, but disqualified by Common Council in 1830, lost appeal to King's Bench 1831.
Scholey, George: distiller; A Dowgate 1805-39; S 1804-5; M 1812 13.
Shadwell, Sir Lancelot: vice-chancellor 1834.
Shaw, Sir James: scrivener; A Portsoken 1798-1831; M.P. City of London 1806-18; president St Bartholomew's Hospital 1806-31.
Sidney, Thomas: girdler; CC Farringdon Without 1843-4; A Billingsgate 1844-80; S 1844-5; M 1853-5; master Girdlers' Co. 1849; M.P. Stafford 1847-52, 1860-5.
Smith, John: bowyer; CC Portsoken 1814-31.

Stacy, George: goldsmith; CC Aldersgate Within 1833-52.
Steuart, Robert: M.P. Haddington, Dunbar, North Berwick, Lauder, Jedburgh 1835, 1837.
Stuart-Wortley, the Honourable James: recorder 1850; solicitor general 1856; M.P. Halifax 1835, Buteshire 1842, 1847, 1852, 1857.
Sutton, the Right Honourable Sir Charles Manners: speaker of House of Commons 1833-5, failed to be re-elected 1835.

Thompson, William: ironmonger; A Cheap 1821-54; S 1822-3; M 1828-9; master Ironmongers' Co. 1829 1841; M.P. Callington 1820-6, City of London 1826-32, Sunderland 1833-41; Westminster 1841-54.
Thorp, John Thomas: draper; CC Aldgate 1812-17; A Aldgate 1817-35; S 1815-16; M 1820-1, elected 1831 but did not serve; M.P. City of London 1818-20.

Venables, William: stationer; A Queenhithe 1821-40; S 1821-2; M 1825-6; master Stationers' Co. 1824-5; M.P. City of London 1831-2.
Vivian, Sir Robert John Hussey; general in Madras infantry, director of East India Company 1855.

Waithman, Robert: framework knitter; CC Farrington Without 1795-1818; A Farrington Without 1818-33; M 1823-4; master Framework Knitters' Co. 1815-16; candidate for Chamberlain 1831; M.P. City of London 1818, 1826, 1831.
Walton, William: goldsmith; CC Aldersgate Without 1821-37.
Ward, Thomas: shipwright; S 1829-30; candidate for A Broad Street 1831.
Ward, William: musician; M.P. City of London 1826-31, withdrew 1831, candidate 1835; director Bank of England 1817-1837.
Whalley, Sir Samuel St Swithin Burden: M.P. Marylebone 1833, 1837.
Wheelton, John: S 1839-40.
Whippey, Benjamin: a saddler in North Audley Street, Grosvenor Square c 1797 to whom Sir Peter Laurie was apprenticed.
White, James: weaver; A Bassishaw 1835-41; M.P. Plymouth 1857, Brighton 1860-74.
Williams, Sir James: goldsmith; S 1821; candidate for A, Bridge 1821.
Wilson, Samuel: weaver; A Castle Baynard 1831-53, Bridge Without 1853-71; S 1833-4, M 1838-9; upper bailiff Weavers' Co. 1833, 1847, 1864.
Wilson, Thomas: spectaclemaker; M.P. City of London 1818-26, candidate 1835.
Winchester, Henry: cutler; A Vintry 1826, 1829-38; S 1826-7; M 1824-5; masters Cutlers' Co. 1829-30; M.P. Maidstone 1830; president St Thomas' Hospital 1835-8.

Wire, David Williams: innholder and girdler; CC Walbrook 1832-51; A Walbrook 1851-60, S 1853-4; M 1858-9; master Girdlers' Co. 1859.
Wood, Sir Matthew: fishmonger; CC Cripplegate Without 1802-7, deputy 1806; A Cripplegate 1807-43; S 1809-10; M 1815-17; prime warden Fishmongers' Co. 1834-6; M.P. City of London 1817-43.
Wood, Thomas: framework knitter; CC Cordwainer 1828-35, deputy 1833; A Cordwainer 1835-47; S 1830-9; master Framework Knitters' Co. 1837-8; clerk of justices at Guildhall 1848-55.
Wood, John: musician; CC Aldersgate 1837-62.
Woodthorpe, Henry: town clerk for City 1825-42.